POEMS

Frontispiece:

"The Cliff Path to Portheras Cove, Cornwall"

From an oil painting by Doris M. Connor

(See page 63)

CONTENTS BY FIRST LINES

DEDICATION

JUVENILIA (SCHOOLBOY VERSE)

UNDERGRADUATE POEMS

WARTIME POEMS

POEMS FOR DORIS

LATER POEMS

REFLECTIONS

To DORIS

With All My Love

A Valentine
    I send to you;
For, line by line,
A Valentine
Can Love enshrine –
    True Love that, through
A Valentine,
    I send to you.

TO AN EARLY LAMB

The suns of springtime saw you come
    While the winter winds still blew,
To depart again in the driving rain
    Or live with the hardy few.

Poor little lamb – too early born!
    Shivering, nestling low,
That your mother's side may shield and hide
    Your own from the icy blow.

Poor little feet, drawn in so close,
    So eager to dance to spring!
Fierce rainstorms greet you, little feet,
    With a cold, bleak everything.

Poor little body, with soft white fluff
    Untarnished as yet by age!
From breezes cool you are warm in wool –
    But not from the winter's rage!

Poor little head with the wee black face,
    So helpless and frightened and cold!
Those eyes that look forth on a windswept Earth
    Should see naught but the sheltered fold.

But not in vain, little early lamb,
    Is your feeble, despairing bleat!
The shepherd has come to carry you home
    To comfort and food and heat;

And, safe and sound in the shepherd's hut,
    No changes can weather bring
Till your little feet the dawn may greet
    With the children of warmer spring.

THE SONG OF TIME

Ye defy me! Ye defy me! Foolish mortals,
　Ye have thwarted me – but only for a day!
I will come a-creeping through your massive portals!
　I will sap the power of your great array!
I will raze your turrets low amid the sun-scorched grass!
　There shall not a single pillar say me nay!
You may thwart, but cannot vanquish, what I bring to pass –
The steady, slow, sure conquest of Decay!

You may polish up your metal till you've banished
　Every tarnished inroad that denotes my sway;
You may rub till every trace of it has vanished,
　And rest content that you have won the fray –
But I will have my vengeance on your burnished brass!
　When I bid the raindrops, "Tarnish!" – they'll obey.
You may thwart, but cannot vanquish, what I bring to pass –
　The steady, slow, sure conquest of Decay!

"In the desert stands the Sphinx, that down the ages
　Has met your wrath unflinchingly," you say.
"It can face the mighty sandstorm when it rages.
　It has stood, is standing, and shall stand for aye."
It will stand – till it has weathered to a shapeless mass;
　And even then my vengeance shall not stay!
You may thwart, but cannot vanquish, what I bring to pass –
　The steady, slow, sure conquest of Decay!

ENVOI

Bar your strongest doors against me, I will splinter them as glass!
　Resist my depredations as you may.
You may thwart, but cannot vanquish, what I bring to pass –
　The steady, slow, sure conquest of Decay!

THE PREY OF THE DESERT

We have no word of him. We cannot tell
   What time he died or where he now is laid;
   If his last thoughts were homeward turned, or strayed
Over the wide earth that he knew so well.
Haply, amid the noonday heat he fell
   And the soft sand a shallow covering made,
   A tomb as restless as the sea, to shade
A roving, restless spirit's empty shell.

Perhaps God heard a prayer in that last hour
   Ere thirst o'erwhelmed him in the wilderness
      And raised his soul upon His healing rod.
   Perhaps – but he is lost and we but guess;
We shall not know till we, too, journey far
   And from the sands of Time are borne to God.

FAME

When cavemen slew the mastodon
    They bore his tusks away
To carve their crude epistles on
    And celebrate the day.
Now, who they were and what they said
    Are equally obscure –
But that the mastodon is dead
    Is very, very sure!

And Man, through all the length of years
    'Twixt savages and sages,
Has written down his hopes and fears
    To please succeeding ages.
"Lest at some future time," he says,
    "My name may not be known,
I'll carve my own unstinted praise
    On rocks and bits of bone."

When Caesar crushed the Gallic tribes
    He made the matter known.
His soldiers' valour he describes –
And, most of all, his own.
And many folk since Caesar's time
    Have filled up great archives
With tales of virtue and of crime:
    The records of their lives.

For Man's desires have ever been
    Coined in the self-same mint;
He carves his deeds; he paints his scene;
    He wriggles into print –
And all, that other little men
    May know his little name!
His toil he deems rewarded when
    He gains his little fame!

Yes, Man will build, as Man has built,
  Like a child by the sea at play,
Whose castles stand in a world of sand
  Till Time sweeps all away.

EPITAPH

Sir Philip Sidney – here he lies,
　With no more songs to sing;
The warrior has found his Prize,
　The courtier his King.

Here in his grave he long has slept,
　He who was these – and more:
A gentleman, whose name was kept
　Unstained in peace and war.

SONNET

Come, for the golden sun has reached the hill.
Slowly, wearily will it disappear,
Fallen from the face of evening, as a tear
Of some fair mermaid trembles and is still
While all around the placid waters thrill.
So do the clouds about the darkening sphere
Blush in its glorious warmth while it is near
And then fade far into the starry chill.

Now is the whole earth quiet, and the birds
Flock in their marshalled thousands to repose;
The flowers fold up their petals; butterflies,
Like small illumined manuscripts, now close;
And I? – I needs must sit and play with words
Writ in the firelight dancing in my eyes.

SONNET

Today is passing, as the rest have passed,
    And what have I accomplished? Have I wrought
    Some mighty harmony? Some lofty thought?
I have but loitered – and the hours ebb fast.
Shall I make something beautiful at last?
    Oft have I tried it, but the mind that ought
    To have roamed in its own music was distraught
By petty, daily troubles, that have massed
And, when I dreamt, have clogged my memory.
    Am I but made to labour and depart
        And do no more than many more have done,
And be no more than many more shall be,
    Who plan great deeds, make many a hopeful start,
        And at the sunset have accomplished none?

SONNET

Here by the chillèd waters stoop and sip
   And watch the bubbles, winking merrily
   Like stars within a silver galaxy,
Flow with enchanted swiftness to thy lip,
Or – like an ash-tree's seeds held in the grip
   Of fresh, light winds – float ever on to thee,
   Touching thee in their childish gaiety
And flying out of reach by soar or dip.

See in these chillèd waters, dim-outlined,
   Thy face transfigured, and thy billowy dress
     Borne like a formless wave from reed to reed,
   As though the stream has deemed thy loveliness
Too great in thy small frame to rest confined
     While all its shady margins stand in need.

FOR MY MOTHER'S BIRTHDAY

Lo! The October leaves are falling down
    And winter threatens in the chilly air.
Soon will the ground be all a dusky brown
    And all these noble trees stand stiff and bare.

Behold, but grieve not, for within a year
    Another foliage will greet the sun,
Another summer's sky will shimmer here,
    Another flock of lambs will sport and run.

Think this, thy birthday in the autumn time,
    Has watched the baby flowers of spring laid by
To sleep awhile; and read in this my rhyme
    The hope that under many an April sky

Thou mayest wander still by hill and lake
And greet thy baby wards as they awake.

THE FISHERMEN
AN EXERCISE IN DACTYLIC RHYTHM

Whispering fearfully,
   Leaves in the night,
Why do ye tearfully
   Mourn for the light?
Whence all this misery?
   Is he not gone
To return cheerfully
   Soon, at the dawn?

Over in Fairyland,
   Down by the lake,
Where the tall rushes stand,
   Where the reeds shake –
There mend the fishermen
   Gossamer nets,
Small elfin fishers, when-
   E'er the sun sets.

Are these your enemies? –
   Tearing you down
Till ye are, by degrees,
   All dead and brown?
Till ye are curled and
   Ready to float
Far from the shadow-land,
   Each as a boat?

What do they seek to find
   Out on the lake?
How can their meshes bind
   Aught that they take? –
This they are trawling for,
   All the night through,
While on the misty shore
   Gathers the dew:

Moonbeams their meshes take,
    Out there beyond –
Beams that some sprite will make
    Shine from her wand.
Trawl away, little elves,
    Out there afar,
Gathering for yourselves
    Light from a star!

But, as ye carelessly
    Drift on your leaf,
Think how a ravished tree
    Murmurs in grief.

TO A SQUIRREL

The leaves are brown again; the autumn sky
  Is grey and sad; and everywhere around
  Acorns and wingèd seeds are to be found,
Seeking beneath the loam a place to lie
And sleep, till in the spring they rise again
  As little, would-be trees. The only sound
    I hear is plashing rain
  And a wee frightened robin's rustling flight.
And here we stand, O squirrel, you and I,
  Each held entrancèd by the other's sight!

There's many a lovely woman would desire
  Your rich, brown fur on such a chilly day.
  Perhaps you think that I may take away
Your winter coat? – but no; all I require
Is your companionship a little while;
  For I am weary, and would gladly stay
    To watch you hoard your pile
  Of beech nuts underneath a fallen tree,
As man stacks peat to feed his winter's fire –
  And yet you will not move, for fear of me!

Gone! Gone as quickly as a wingèd thing
  To where the twigs can hardly bear your weight!
  Leaping from tree to tree at such a rate
That I cannot keep near you, following!
Chattering, scuffling, digging deep your claws
  Into the upright bark, trusting your fate
    To leaves, rather than pause!
  O squirrel, squirrel, why this mad career?
I meant no harm, when in my wandering
  I came upon you, busy gathering here...

Gone far away, a glinting russet mass!
  Perhaps I shall not see him till the sun
  Of spring assures him that ill times are done,
And he slips down, half sleeping, to the grass.
Farewell, then, little squirrel, for this year!
  I shall remember you when, one by one,
    The crocus buds appear,
  And look again, hoping to find you tame,
Hoping I shall not fright you as I pass
  But watch at will your merry, scampering game.

SONNET

Smile once again! The sullen, wintry day
  Has left the whole world drooping. Think not thou
  That those bright smiles are wasted, e'en though now
In all the earth they find no answering ray;
For afterwards, when thou art gone away,
  The labourer will remember at his plough;
  The trees will whisper, bending bough to bough,
And in their leaves thy loveliness shall stay.

Smile once again, that I may gather in
  The dazzling splendour of thy countenance
    To solace me when I am far from thee.
Haply the knowledge that I once could win,
  Only by asking it, thine own dear glance
    May spur me on to final victory.

THE ZOOLOGY CLASS

With limbs extended, flat upon its back,
   The dead frog lies, all ready for the knife
   Of him who stifled its innocuous life
To come again and on its corpse to track

The pulseless arteries in every limb.
   The little trunk lies open, pinned apart,
   And tiny organs, framed by God's own art,
Lie stark and quivering in confusion grim.

Is it just squeamishness, wasted sympathy,
   Makes me abhor this needless sacrifice?
      Perhaps – yet better far my wavering
Than that I should go forward callously.
   A surgeon's skill – it is not worth the price
   Of all compassion for a little thing.

ELEGY ON THE DEATH OF THE AXOLOTL

IN OUR BIOLOGY LABORATORY

The ancients did not know it. Aristotle,
Homer, Lucretius, Virgil, had they seen
This curious tadpole, would, I feel, have been
Tempted, like us, to put it in a bottle;
But would they, pray, have tried to cram its throttle
With more food than the creature could contain?
Such have we done – and hence my dismal strain
To mourn the passing of our Axolotl.

A very lively prisoner was he,
And of the captive tadpoles I have known
In point of size unquestionably first.
He used to watch us in Zoology,
His ugly head just peeping round a stone.
Not any more. Our Axolotl's burst.

THE WALK

Another stone? Another stick to find?
   You haven't found the last one that I threw –
   Because you romped ahead, thinking you knew
Where it would fall, and never looked behind!
Have you no thoughts inside your doggy mind
   But finding other fields to squeeze into,
   And begging till I throw more sticks to you
Or call a sharp, "To heel!" – and feel unkind?

It is your chief delight – this evening game;
   The only price you ask for all the joy
      And boisterous welcomes that you keep for me.
   If I begrudged this hour I would destroy
Your happiness – wee Jock, while yet I claim
      Your friendship, sure I give it willingly!

CHANT ROYAL OF THE ROSE

In England, centuries ago,
  Two princes, so the annals say,
Disputed bitterly, to show
  Why each should wield the royal sway.
They passed the courtly gardens through
(Each with his friends – a chosen few)
  And saw the roses, red or white,
  Ranged like two armies opposite;
    Between them had not yet been bred
A mid-way blossom to unite –
    A motley rose of white and red.

Said York, "The very flowers, lo,
  Two rival colours here array!
I choose the white rose, for I know
  No crimson Error there can stay."
He culled a rose of milky hue
From the barbèd stem on which it grew
  And waved it in the courtiers' sight.
  "Beneath this emblem will I fight
    And win the English throne!" he said.
(How England needed in her plight
    A motley rose of white and red!)

Proud Lancaster responded slow:
  "Let York his pale white rose display!
For me the blood-red rose shall grow,
  For with their blood my foes shall pay
Till, deathly pale, my peace they sue."
His jewelled dagger forth he drew –
  Before their eyes it glinted bright –
  And a red rose was severed quite
    And gathered from its garden bed...
Years were to pass, ere met the light
    A motley rose of white and red –

Long years of conflict and of woe,
  When son and father met to slay,
When England was both friend and foe
  And ancient glories passed away.
For years the rival trumpets blew;
For years the rival banners flew;
  The jaws of war were clenchèd tight,
  And England sank within their bite –
    How comes it, now she lifts her head? –
  Lo! yonder waves a blossom slight,
    A motley rose of white and red.

York sleeps, and Lancaster, where snow
  Has often visited their clay.
Now, where the Red Rose pennons flow,
  A young Prince rideth forth today.
Yet here the White Rose rideth too –
Princess of York, his helpmate true.
  How glorious is their blended might!
  Now fades the enmity and spite,
    And from the ground where thousands bled
  There blossoms, like a friendly sprite,
    A motley rose of white and red.

ENVOI

My lady! Lo, I send to you
This flower of peace, that buds anew
  When every winter takes his flight
  And summer trembles to her height.
    So be your joys replenishèd,
  Like the fair rose of which I write –
    A motley rose of white and red!

THE POSTULANT

Take me, break me, O God, if there be need!
  Temper me on the searing coals of pain;
    Stay not the blows of sorrow, for they rain
To shape my soul. Not for relief I plead;
For my world is shattered, Lord, and I am freed
  From hope of self – set free to live again
    But as Thy weapon. Forge me not in vain!
Firm in Thy grasp, let me thy purpose speed!

My sole ambition, Lord, to do Thy will;
  My sole possession, Lord, Thy love for me;
    My only pride, that Thou hast made me Thine –
So let me live, so let me serve Thee still;
  So let me die, shaping Thy World-to-be,
    And, dying, live graven in Thy Design!

THE LAND OF LEAFONY

This legendary country is said to lie beneath the waters of Lough
Neagh. The plot is taken from the late M.G. Crawford's *Legendary
Stories of the Carlingford Lough District.*

i

The golden pomp of day draws to its close,
And, etched in ebony against the sky,
The King and all his train are wending home.
Full many a weary sun, in years gone by,
Has watched them pass, to share in its repose;
But now, with pageant fair and minstrelsy,
The chiefs, the courtiers and the damsels come
Across the shadowy Land of Leafony,
And from the palace hall the expectant music flows.

ii

For was not this a day made glorious
By plighted troth of marriage and of love,
Wherein a noble Princess bows her head,
Humbly yet radiantly to approve
The manly Prince of a far-off Royal House?
Sing, then, ye maidens! Dance the night away!
Feast till the new sun rises; let the red
Wine flow in brimming goblets – for today,
Sought out and won, our Princess takes her leave of us...

iii

She takes her leave; but, fleeter far than she,
The birds that nest in Leafony have gone.
The fox, the coney and the panting frog
Seek out new haunts. The grey wolf and the fawn
Alike are fled; and, straining to be free,
The horses champ, the kine jostle and low,
Fearing they know not what. The faithful dog
Stands with alarmèd head, but will not go
While in the heedless throng his lord holds revelry.

iv

Lo! On the Royal table, gleaming gold,
The sacred fish, drawn from the fairy pool,
Lie decked for the repast – for they are made
Its chiefest glory... and the waters cool
Swirl in their magic spring. It has been told
(In the old foolish story) that should e'er
The riever's hand on these bright fish be laid,
The Land of Leafony, that blooms so fair,
And all its warm young life, shall icy doom enfold.

v

It is just a quaint old tale, that lingers yet
In yonder hutment by the palace wall
Where the young peasant and his comely wife
Sit by the fire, and let their voices fall
Lest, in his cot, their baby wake and fret –
A tale of how, when first Clan Eochy came
To Leafony, and after bitter strife
Drove out the Danaan folk with sword and flame,
An o'erwhelmed but crafty people sought to pay its debt;

vi

For they were wise, the people of the land,
And steeped in all the arts of sorcery.
Now, in the caves of the surrounding hills,
They schemed and laboured, that on Leafony
A subtle spell might fall at their command.
Soon all her wells were dried. Of clouds, not one
Crossed the encircling mountains. The small rills
That swelled to make her rivers ceased to run.
Famine and thirst and death stole near on either hand.

vii

And Eochy, father of the conquering race,
On whose great shoulders rested now the doom
Of kindred and of children, wandered on,
Wrapped in his thoughts, to where the great hills loom
Around his country – searching for a space
Still unenchanted, longing in his heart
Among these highland springs to find just one
Still green with moisture, whence there yet might start
A stream to save his people and their dwelling-place.

viii

Upon his path it chanced there met with him
A bent old man, who still contrived to wear
The semblance of a prince in voice and mien.
He, pausing, spoke: "King Eochy, let your care
Fall from your shoulders, for there yet shall brim
Springs full of flowing water. I have skill –
Born of a Fairy who was once the Queen
Of Leafony – to tap this sacred hill
And draw mysterious waters from its caverns dim.

ix

"And I am fain to do this; for the clan
Whom you have conquered linger in my caves
And wreak with their enchantments desecration.
But mark my one condition: 'neath the waves
Of this bright flood, safe from the hand of man,
My sacred fish must dwell for ever more.
If ever they are snared, then on this nation
And on this land a harsher doom than war
Must fall, a silence greater than when earth began."

x

Such was the quaint old story which the boy
Told softly to his wife beside the fire;
And, as he ceased, there knocked upon the door
A bent old man, in sombre grey attire,
Whose gleaming eyes seemed yearning to destroy
With evil light whate'er they gazed upon;
And in his hand a grey-leafed branch he bore,
A plant that grew in Leafony alone.
"O Man," the stranger said, "let me your hearth enjoy."

xi

"Through all this city have I come, in quest
Of shelter for the night, but there was none;
And I am weary – ay, and broken-hearted."
Almost the frightened peasant had begun
To close the door upon this eerie guest,
Yet paused, for as the stranger turned away
The girl sped forth to him ere he departed.
"Whoe'er thou art," she said, "here shalt thou stay.
Thou art old and weary; come, for here are peace and rest."

xii

"Blest be that heart whose bounty does not cease
In fear of the unknown!" the stranger said.
"O daughter, thou and thine alone shall know
Deliverance from this valley of the dead!
My sacred fish are stolen! – and from their place
The doom of Leafony is welling up!
Take up thy babe; follow me where I go,
Ere yet the waters brim their earthen cup
And Leafony is drowned with all its hapless race..."

xiii

From o'er the hills a horse comes speedily,
Spurred by Clan Eochy's sentry; he has seen
The waters rolling downwards on his home.
Swift through the streets he flies, swift o'er the green,
Crying, "Awake, Clan Eochy! Rise and flee!"
Around his charger's hooves the waters swirl,
Around his thighs the gathering waves of doom...
And king and gillie, princess and peasant girl
Sleep in eternal sleep beneath the restless sea.

THE MOUSE – A RONDEAU

A little mouse, one winter's day,
Into the kitchen came to stay.
  In cautious little spurts it stole
  Behind the scuttle for the coal
To wait till Cook had gone away;

Then up it scampered to the tray
Where cakes and scones and crumpets lay –
  No risk would keep from such a goal
    A little mouse!

When Cook returned, what *did* she say?
With fright and anger and dismay
  I fear she was beyond control;
  But, safe within a secret hole,
Slept, like an infant tired of play,
    A little mouse.

SUBURBIA

Each time I come across a spotless car
   I think of Thompson and his Austin Ten –
   Thompson, and Smith, and all the other men
I know, whose home-from-home is not the 'bar';
But look outside each garage – there they are!
   Wielding the spanner deftly as a pen,
   Making the coachwork shine and shine again...
And in the end they never travel far.

But Thompson is the best (or worst?) of all.
   He talks of nothing else but plugs and gears.
Poor Mrs Thompson always finds her hall
   Reeking of petrol, splashed with oily smears.
Sometimes, I think, she'd rather see him crawl
   Home from the pub, for once, in maudlin tears.

KILLYLEAGH

"There is not a louse in Killyleagh" – from the evidence of the School
Medical Officer at Downpatrick Petty Sessions.

The Russian, it is said,
Harbours lice within his bed;
The Scotch are scratching nearly all the day;
And it's rumoured that in Eire
Fleas are not exactly rare-ah,
But there's not a louse alive in Killyleagh!

There's a quantity of fleas
On the average Portuguese;
There are bugs abroad all over USA;
A variety of vermin
Can be cultured on the German –
But there's not a louse alive in Killyleagh!

Not a cow need scrape its hide,
Not a sheep be dipped and dried,
Not a cur need pause to scratch an itch away –
For we've made a powerfu' slaughter
Wi' a brush an' soap an' water,
And there's not a louse alive in Killyleagh,
In Killyleagh –
AND THERE'S NOT A LOUSE ALIVE IN KILLYLEAGH!

WAITING IN THE HALL

"There's time enough to catch the train!" –
In accents of reproachful pain
    My warnings are rejected flat.
    There's time to change, to choose a hat –
And all remonstrances are vain!

I wonder how I stand the strain.
Look at the clock! I'll shout again:
    Darling, what are you playing at?…
      "There's time enough!"

It seems that in a woman's brain
Unworldly instincts still remain;
    Angelic? – Well, we'll call them that;
    Strayed from *some* Heavenly habitat
Where, in Eternity, it's plain
      There's time enough!

VARIATIONS ON A THEME

Question: Why did the hen cross the road?
Answer: To get to the other side.

1. LIMERICK

I once asked a hen why it tried
To cross over the road. It replied,
  "There are some things I do
  For no reason – like you.
I just crossed to the opposite side."

2. TRIOLET

Across the road
  The other side
Distinctly showed.
Across the road
The chicken strode
  Because it spied,
Across the road,
  The other side.

3. SONNET

Across the tarmacadam, panic-struck,
    Scurried the hen, its silly neck and wings
    Making a futile storm of flutterings.
Beneath my very wheels it seemed to 'duck',
And plunged to safety in the grass and muck
    That lined the verge. "What idiotic things
    Are hens!" I thought, resentful that fate brings
Their crass stupidity such unearned luck.

One might, indeed, forgive a hen which showed
    Some reason for adventuring far and wide –
An extra feed of grain, to be bestowed
    On those who flapped across to be supplied –
But there was none. The hen had crossed the road –
    Had crossed MY road! – to reach the other side.

4. RONDEAU

My little hen, without a glance
To see if any circumstance,
  Such as the traffic in the lane,
  Ought to have made you think again
Before attempting to advance –

You strode across, as in a trance.
Was it some poultry farm romance
  Which fully occupied your brain,
    My little hen?

Or were you seeking to enhance,
By thus ignoring all mischance,
  A studied pose of high disdain?
  You crossed in safety – but 'tis vain
To count on such deliverance,
    My little hen!

5. VILLANELLE

Behold a hen which tried,
  Across the thoroughfare,
To reach the other side.

Although the road was wide,
  And danger everywhere,
Behold a hen which tried

To take it in its stride,
  And with a jaunty air
To reach the other side.

Alas, alas for pride!
  When other folk are ware
Behold a hen which tried! –

Behold a hen which died,
  Seeking without due care
To reach the other side.

'Tis better far to bide
In safety, while you're there...
Behold a hen which tried
To reach the other side!

6. BALLADE

I sing the hen! – the flustered, feathered hen!
  Whose praises, in the books that I have read,
Have rarely flowed beneath the Poet's pen.
  Oh, base ingratitude! – for it has bred
  The quill he dips; its feathers must be shed
    Ere he can write at all. Therefore with pride
  I sing the useful hen, of whom 'tis said:
    It crossed the road to reach the other side.

And not the Poet only, now and then
  Has cause to thank the hen; for in his bed
The sluggard, lying in till half past ten,
  Upon a feathered pillow rests his head.
  The little hen that pillow furnishèd –
    And probably his breakfast, too, supplied,
  Because, to lay the egg on which he fed,
    It crossed the road to reach the other side.

He gives no thanks. But Cook has blessed it when,
  With strange ingredients around her spread,
She kneads and bakes within her private den.
  Her hour of triumph would indeed be fled
  Without her eggs – what could she use instead?
    Alas! that one so useful should collide
  With fate, when, by a reckless impulse led,
    It crossed the road to reach the other side.

ENVOI

Princess! Receive my hen, for it is dead.
    Roast it and eat it; 'twas for thee it died;
For, as my steed towards thy palace sped,
    It crossed the road to reach the other side.

ENGLAND, 1942

(WITH APOLOGIES TO WORDSWORTH)

Bacon! Would there were more of thee today!
Old England longs for thee; she is the scene
Of wartime rationing. Sugar, margarine,
Eggs, and the luscious fruits from far away
Have lost, alas! the plentiful array
  Of pre-war catering. We are growing lean.
  Oh cheer us up! Make us what we have been
When on our plates ham, pork or rashers lay!

Thy source was once a Pig, and looked the part.
  He had a girth that rocked him on his feet –
  Like a barràge balloon, but more replete;
    So did he thrive, enlarging more and more
By refuse-scavenging; and yet this art
    The richest bacon in his hide did store!

BIRTHDAY GREETINGS FOR MY A.T.S. SECRETARY, 1943

Attend, ye Muses, in that strange retreat
Of laudatory verse – the M.I. Room!
Without your aid what poet would presume
To lay his simple tribute at the feet
Of her who is its Queen? Shall I compete
With Time, the Great Artificer, from whom
She has received a year of golden bloom,
And is with all his glories now replete?

What shall I praise, then? – the effectiveness
With which she marshals Army documents?
Her speed and deftness at stenography? –
Ah, vain were the attempt! The A.T.S.,
For charm, for skill, for comeliness, presents
No damsel to be matched with Marjorie!

(M.I. Room = Medical Inspection Room, the combined office and
surgery of an army doctor.)

SPENSERIAN STANZAS ON THE OFFICERS' AND LADIES' CRICKET MATCH, BENENDEN, KENT, 12 JULY 1944.

The 105th Military General Hospital mustered in Benenden before setting up its tents near Bayeux after the Normandy landing. The officers who played in this cricket match were all doctors, except for the Quartermaster ('Q'). The majority of the ladies were Queen Alexandra nursing sisters, but there were also two ambulance drivers, two physiotherapists (classified as civilians) and one doctor (Capt. Potter). Play was interrupted several times when flying bombs ('doodle-bugs') passed overhead.

i

Ere yet the Oval had achieved its fame
Full many a jolly cricket match was played,
With no elaborate rules to spoil the game.
How gaily then the buxom dairymaid,
Facing the ploughboy's bowling unafraid,
Guarded her three-legg'd stool till, letting fire,
She smashed the kitchen window and, dismayed,
Dived headlong for the haystack or the byre,
Or any place to hide in from the farmer's ire.

ii

Those were the days; yet here, in Benenden,
We have recaptured something of their fun;
For here a troupe of damsels played the men
Of 'One-O-Five' – and very nearly won!
Attend and hear what feats of skill were done,
What bowling knocked beyond the boundary line,
What batsmen stumped or caught when scarce begun –
This were a theme for greater powers than mine,
Yet it is mine to sing, and one I'll not resign!

iii

'Twas on an afternoon of mid-July,
As peaceful as the 'Doodle-bugs' allowed,
When this enthralling test of mastery
Was held, in presence of a wondering crowd.

See, then, the Officers, how – rashly proud! –
They thought to demonstrate superior skill;
The Ladies, too, demure but quite uncowed –
How resolute their stance! How firm their will
To humble and outmatch these lords invincible!

iv

The batsmen came, the Ladies first of all;
And Sisters Smith and Cleve stepped boldly out.
Alas, poor Cleve! – hers was an early fall;
But Sister Smith played on, dauntless and stout,
Her partner now Miss Wright (and she, no doubt,
Would add at least a fifty to the score) –
Ah no! She, too, fell victim to the rout:
She hit the ball indeed; she watched it soar –
But Captain Ross reached out – and she was in no more!

v

Then, with her laurels won, Miss Smith was bowled.
Smeaton and Corfield to the wicket came;
The score rose steadily, and then twofold
Disaster fell upon them by the same
Mischance; they hit the balls with perfect aim,
But Colonel Denvir caught one as it fell,
The other, Major Gillam – what a shame
To lose two batsmen who were hitting well!
But such is life, that saddens every tale we tell.

vi

Then Captain Petronella Potter strode,
Tight-lipped and resolute, to take their place;
And soon the total on the scoreboard showed
How good a bat the fielders now must face.
At last, when all were panting with the pace,
The worthy Captain missed; the bails flew high;
The fielders, thankful for a breathing space,
Clapped to the echo as she passed them by
But hoped the next girl in had not as keen an eye.

vii

Fond hope – with Sister Hitchcock next to bat!
She struck out right and left with might and main.
It is not, therefore, to be wondered at
That scoring mounted rapidly again
Till she was caught, after a hectic reign,
Dethroned by Colonel Hughes. Then (tragic fate!)
Poor Sister Whiting, hitting out in vain,
Was bowled; for luck turns fickle soon or late
And oft the weak survive where conflicts crush the great.

viii

With Sister Robinson the Ladies' side
Revived again, for seven runs she made;
And Driver Martin, hitting far and wide,
Seemed bent on putting all into the shade –
But all too soon her valiant course was stayed,
Caught by that tousled Highlander, Mackay;
And Driver Workman, who had scarcely played,
Perforce must leave to keep her company.
The Ladies were dismissed – yet not ingloriously.

ix

Now came the Officers to bat in turn,
And Captain Murray (with his new moustache!)
Frowned at the bowler with an eye so stern
That few could think of him as being rash.
Yet, before long, he made a foolish dash
And left his partner, Captain Lees, to bear
The penalty; the distant wickets crash,
And Captain Lees, still several yards from there,
Wheeled in disgust – run out – and marched off head-in-air.

x

But Captain Ross's was a happier fate;
For he and Captain Murray each had scored
Full fifteen runs when they retired in state.
The Officers could therefore well afford
To lose poor Richards by a shot which soared

Into Gwen Martin's strong and fatal clasp...
Here let us pause; for I must now record
A deed whose motives few could claim to grasp;
A villainy so deep that one can only gasp:–

xi

The Officer Commanding 'One-O-Five',
Denvir the Dauntless, to the wicket came,
Resolved to make the batting come alive;
And Captain Henry – dare I speak that name? –
Deliberate, and quite devoid of shame,
Ran out the noble Colonel! In amaze
At his abrupt dismissal from the game
The warrior left the pitch with eyes ablaze
And muttered threats of vengeance on ensuing days.

xii

Now by this time we all had such a thirst
That when the cricket match adjourned for tea
There was a rush for who-should-get-there-first,
And Captain Henry and his infamy
Were soon forgot, what time the company
Of Officers and Ladies guzzled cake
And in the dance hall chattered merrily
(They ate so much, indeed, in that short break
That most of them deserved to have a tummy-ache).

xiii

Then, to the Unit Band, they tried to dance,
Lurching and pirouetting round the hall.
The cricketers had left them in advance,
And soon the dancers followed, one and all
Intent on keeping track of every ball
And hoping Captain Henry, in his turn,
Would have a swift and ignominious fall.
Alas! Good people, how might they discern
The treason still unhatched? – but they were soon to learn!

xiv

As soon as Colonel Foster, out for one,
Had left the pitch, in toddled Colonel Hughes
To play an expert game of tip and run;
And who knows what a score in ones and twos
He might have made – but by the self-same ruse
Captain McGinty Henry ran him out!
Nor did he try such treason to excuse –
Instead he grinned, and with derisive shout
Pranced up and down the pitch and waved his arms about.

xv

Then Henry's wicket fell – long past its time –
Stumped by a deadly shot from fair Miss Wright,
A fitting punishment to meet his crime.
And now Mackay was in, with all his might
Knocking the bowling almost out of sight
Till Sister Smeaton stopped him once for all:
How temptingly she bowled! He tried to smite
So hard he missed and nearly had a fall –
And down his wicket went before a well-aimed ball.

xvi

And what of Captain Dixon all this while?
Playing a steady innings, neat and true;
By one and one he added to his pile;
He gave no catch, he let no bowling through –
A very cautious cricketer was 'Q'!
And so, when Major Gillam, last to play,
Swung back, and right and left his wicket flew,
The stalwart 'Q' looked round as if to say,
"That is what comes of SWANK – but I'm *not out* today!"

xvii

The Officers were out – but they had won!
By sixty-nine they won, to fifty-four.
But they had had to fight for every run,
And what the Ladies' team had still in store
Was soon revealed, for they renewed the war,

Unbroken by defeat and keen to show
That it was chance which had curtailed their score.
With flashing bats they drove against the foe,
And far away the fielders staggered to and fro.

xviii

Time presses, and I cannot now repeat
Each noble innings that the Ladies played;
But there was scarcely one who did not beat
Her former score. They put into the shade
The fielders' score, and altogether made
More than a hundred runs by twenty-three!
Which proves indeed that but for Fortune's aid
The winners had been vanquished utterly –
Yet when the game is close how grand is victory!

xix

The stumps are drawn at last; my story ends;
And of the summer day remains no trace –
Gone, but not wasted; it was spent with friends.
Henceforth it rests with us not to efface
That fellowship. The war draws near apace.
Another contest now is ours to fight.
Yet, by our comradeship, for this brief space
We have *lived*. We must not hold that bounty light...
Pause, and shake hands, my friends, before we say,
"Good night."

REMEMBRANCE SONNET

We knew them as our comrades. We shall raise
  Heads that are proud with sorrow when men tell
  Of brave young souls who stood and fought and fell
And left to us their heritage of days.
We shall remember, on the paths we blaze,
  The land, the hopes they loved and guarded well.
  We shall be still, touched deeply by the spell
Of gratitude they leave with us always.

The future is not ours to take or squander;
  These comrades of our boyhood, it is theirs.
    Where freedom lives, where poverty is slain,
There shall their spirit dwell, their footsteps wander
  Over our hills, and in our thoroughfares
    Their selfless accents shall be heard again.

VALENTINE AND BIRTHDAY WISHES

To Night Sister, German P.O.W. Ward, Surgical;
May Queen of Elstow.

From the Medical Officer i/c Troops and Reception;
Bard of the Kingdom of Mourne.

Oostende, February 1945

Since what is charming, dear, and what is true
 In one young lovely girl so rarely blend,
 And since the happy hours that I may spend
Here in your company are far too few,
And I too shy, to give you praises due –
 Accept this little sonnet I have penned,
 That every time you read it I may send
My thoughts, my wishes and my dreams to you.

My birthday greetings first: may happy days
 Year after year over your pathway shine;
May friends – true friends – be near in all your ways
 To help and to delight you, lady mine.
Today is mine, and while the moment stays
 I claim you, Doris, for my Valentine!

AUBADE

Waken, darling! Day is here;
Over yonder mountain, clear
Shines the newly-rising sphere.
Waken, darling! From your bed
Raise that little sleepy head.
Fold away the dreams which made,
All night long, a fairy glade
Where your random thoughts could play
While the world in darkness lay.
Open wide those sleepy eyes
To the splendour of the skies,
And see the drowsy world renew,
Flower by flower, its richest hue,
Bespangled with the morning dew.
Gather in your veil of hair –
Kneel beside your bed in prayer –
Bathe, and clothe you, and appear,
Darling, for the day is here!

Then through the garden let us pass,
Treading down the quivering grass,
And underneath the arches go,
Where the rambler roses grow;
Where the fountain sparkles cool
And the goldfish beautiful
Glimmer in the garden pool;
Where the trees on either side
With their boughs reach out to hide
All the earth's sweet comeliness
From the passionate caress
Of the breezes and the bright
Fingers of the morning light.

I will gather for your breast
All the flowers you love the best:
Little pansies, purple, gold
In colour, or the manifold

Clustered polyanthus tops;
Tulips with their moulded cups;
Or frilly blooms of pink and red
That beckon from the garden bed
Where the carnation nods her head;
Orange lilies' proud regalia;
Curled wax petals of the dahlia –
Choose them, dear, this summer morning
Waiting here for your adorning.
Or the rose, the queen of all,
For your bosom shall I cull?
The rose, whose pure and royal grace
Most worthily becomes your face;
Whose hue can match, though not eclipse,
The glory of your cheeks or lips;
Whose buds are steeped in soft perfume
Even as your fragrance fills a room.
Come, my darling, for ere long
The birds will cease their morning song.
Let us wander down the lane,
Listening to their light refrain,
Searching out in hedge and tree
The minstrel of each melody...
O my lady, let us stray
Together all this summer day!

Shall we spend it by the stream
Where the eddies curl and gleam,
Where the cattle stand and dream?
There, outstretched upon the grass,
Shall we watch the hours pass,
While no idle passer-by –
Except the airy butterfly –
Intrudes upon our sanctuary?
Then, where the wind disturbs us least,
Let us unpack our little feast:
Bread and butter, jam, and cheese –

What need have we of luxuries
Whose every want is thus supplied
Down by the river, side by side!

Or is a ramble through the wood
More suited to an errant mood? –
The wood where, at each turn, abound
New mysteries of sight and sound;
Where rabbits pop from underground;
Where, high above, the squirrel swings
From bough to bough as if on wings.
Let us frolic there, or slacken,
Plunging deep amid the bracken,
Glad at heart and reconciled
With the spirit of the wild.

Or shall we take the mountain track?
With panting breath and stooping back
Clambering up from stage to stage
On our self-chosen pilgrimage?
(How light is any task to me
With you to bear me company!)
Till, far beneath, the country lies,
Mile after mile, before our eyes.
Far off, behold the village sleep;
And yonder lies the purple deep,
So far, we cannot hear it moan.
And on the hill we stand alone –
Lords of the hill and of the sky,
Two royal eagles nested high,
A prince and princess – you and I!

Or shall we to the sea go down? –
Not where it sleeps beneath the town,
A placid lake, where little ships
Skim to and fro on pleasure trips;
But where upon the lonely strand
The breakers surge against the land;
Where the seagulls swoop and cry,

Where the stubble-grasses die,
Yielding place to rock and gravel,
Where the seaweeds toss and ravel.
Hand in hand we two will race
To meet the breakers face to face,
And plunge our bodies in the foam
As if we sought to overcome
The slow persistence of the tide
That edges in on either side.
Then, back returning from our swim,
Tingling cool in every limb,
Let us rest, our battles done,
In the bright and burning sun.

Hasten, darling; sleep is best
When the sun has gone to rest.
Then, with all your ardour spent,
You may slumber well content;
And the God whose constant care
Fashioned you and made you fair –
He will watch your sleep, and bless
With health and mirth and loveliness.
But, my lady, it is day!
Hasten, rise, and come away
While the sun is on the hill,
While the birds are singing still,
While, beneath your window, dear,
I am waiting, waiting here.

RONDEAU

My Very Own, when I behold
That radiant face of yours, the mould
Of all the beauty that I see
Decking this earth so royally,
My thoughts swirl upwards uncontrolled;

My heart, so faint, grows strong and bold
With yearning passion to enfold
Your lovely self with mine, to be
My very own.

What though the sages have extolled
The wisest life aloof and cold!
My life must be a mockery
Unless my lady lives with me –
While we are young, when we are old,
My very own.

VILLANELLE

If our lives could never end
  Nor Love's morning disappear
I should greet you as a friend.

Could the centuries extend
And your presence still be near –
If our lives could never end –

Carelessly we then should spend,
  Day by day, the passing year:
I should greet you as a friend.

But upon the way we wend
  Looms an hour we should not fear
If our lives could never end;

And because I comprehend
  All that we might lose, if here
I should greet you as a friend,

Passion wings my hopes, to blend
  Wholly with your being, dear.
If our lives could never end
I should greet you as a friend.

SONNET

The morning sunlight streams across my bed,
And rising hopes on my forebodings fling
A golden light that changes everything.
God, who has made this glorious world, and led
Many a child to happiness, has shed
On you and me the splendour of His spring.
O darling, when I think of Him I sing,
Knowing our needs shall, like the birds, be fed.

Surely He knows our love! Surely He will
On some clear morning take us by the hand
And lead us forth rejoicing, to fulfil
His dearest hope, and ours – that we may stand
As one before Him all our days, until
The skies shall open on His holy land!

SHAKESPEARIAN SONNET

I stand perplexed, my lady, and distressed,
    Doubting each step, yet dreading each delay,
And knowing not how I may serve you best.
    I long to clasp you to my heart today,

To face the sweep of the uncharted years
    Under the inspiration of your love,
Like a benighted traveller, who steers
    By a clear star that guides him from above.

Yet, darling, if my rash and eager heart
    Should lure you from your path to lasting joy,
How like a Vandal should I play my part,
    Approaching beauty only to destroy!

This only through bewilderment I see:
My love for you, dear heart; your love for me.

RONDEAU, WRITTEN AT
PORTHERAS COVE, CORNWALL

If you were here, this lovely scene –
The cornfields quivering, tall and green,
    By summer-scented breezes fanned;
    The white waves breaking on the sand;
Blue sky, where seagulls glide serene;

The ocean, where a golden sheen
Runs like a pathway for a queen –
    Darling, it would be Fairyland
    If you were here!

I know that now you do not lean
Over yon pebbly brook, to glean
    Those yellow blossoms with your hand;
    Yet, Doris, all day long I stand…
And see things… as they might have been
    If you were here.

SONNET

Time passes slowly, darling, day by day;
    And night by night I think of you, and dream
    Until the shadows on my pillow seem
(Touch not, or they will vanish!) to portray
The lovely face that is so far away,
    The lovely girl whose touch was the supreme
    Enchantment of those hours which used to stream
Over our happiness at rest or play.

We did not count them then, but now I see
    Each little moment of our past delight –
        Yearning, yet not in sadness; for, ere long,
Though time returns not, you will come to me,
    Not as a shadow only, in the night,
        Nor as a daydream in my wistful song.

SONNET

My arms are empty, Doris, though I yearn
   To hold you close, to kiss you, and to praise
   Your lovely self in Love's enchanted ways.
Yet, dear, in silence we have come to learn
How through the lonely miles we may discern
   Each other. When I close mine eyes I gaze
   Into your eyes; I pause, and phrase by phrase
Remembered echoes of your voice return.

In what far country, dearest, do we meet
   In silence and with eyes fast closed – the air
      Stilled with expectant love, and all around
Bright memories, and hopes with pattering feet,
   Welcoming us? Oh, darling, unaware
      Surely we stand with God on holy ground!

SONNET

Under the radiance of this starry sky
  The darling of my heart lies stilly sleeping.
  How blind the night! How cold the shadows, creeping
Over her lovely form without a sigh!
Over her head the moon goes heedless by.
  Night sees not, nor the night winds idly sweeping,
  How beautiful she is, whom to their keeping
Fate would surrender, yet to me deny!

O envious Fate! Boast not of villainy
  Though between Doris and my arms is spun
A web of miles of the unfriendly sea.
  By Time, deft-fingered, it shall be undone,
For unto Time and all Eternity
  I and my best-belovèd are as one!

SONNET – TO DORIS ON HER PORTRAIT

Of beauties that are formed by Nature's lore –
   Whether revealed in girlhood's comely face
   Or in the body's youth and strength and grace –
Darling, of these you have abundant store;
Yet here, this evening, as I stand before
   Your portrait, lost in rapture, I can trace
   A loveliness too deep to find a place
With outward beauty in a listed score.

Oh! that mine eyes were opened wide to see
   That lovely soul no portrait can impart
      Although its light illumines every line!
Courage is here, faith and sincerity,
   And gentleness, and gaiety of heart
      Here in one lovely girl – and she is mine!

VALENTINE SONNET

Darling, behold once more my Valentine,
   In recollection of our dreams come true!
   A year ago our love was only new,
A glimmering hope that scarcely dared to shine
Over me, as I fashioned, line by line,
   My first, shy song for you. The words were few,
   But they were tokens of a love which grew
Till it has glorified your life and mine.

Greater than all our hopes, than all our dreaming,
   Is now the happiness that fills our life
      As this new birthday comes to you – and me.
Lovely you seemed; far lovelier than your seeming
   I have found. I know you, Doris – my sweet wife
      These few months past and all the Years To Be!

SONNET

How shall I tell how beautiful you are,
   My darling? – now, when you are all my own;
   Now when, long since, my love for you has grown
Beyond the compass of my verse so far
That all my words of praise can only mar
   Its greatness? Doris, you have freely shown
   All that my heart can hold; yet, still unknown,
Your beauty gleams beyond me like a star.

O my belovèd, mine can never be
   The rapturous song of poets or of seers;
Yet, in such joy as you have brought to me,
   Hushed like my own, their music disappears.
Therefore I gaze in silent ecstasy
   Until mine eyes grow dim with quivering tears.

CHANT ROYAL

The noblest words have all been said,
   The sweetest songs made long ago.
What Muse shall I invoke instead
   In praise of her to whom I owe
The tribute of a love divine
For all her heart has brought to mine?...
   Belovèd, though my task is vain,
   Your gentleness will not disdain
      These little words of song I pour
   Upon your path, my Sovereign,
      Whom I will love for ever more.

What shall I sing – your small, dark head?
   Your eyes – what words can make them glow?
Darling, I never dreamt or read
   Of love to match the love we know:
As tender as a Valentine;
As bright as Heaven, with stars that shine;
   As distant as the lark's refrain –
   Yet filled with joy akin to pain,
      So close love comes. I need not soar
   To find you. Here your head has lain,
      Whom I will love for ever more.

Whom I will love when years have sped
And touched your curls with wisps of snow,
Like daisies where the lawn is spread –
   Unsought, but lovely where they show.
Some far-off day you must resign
Your flawless youth, yet need not pine,
   Whose inward beauty knows no stain.
   O darling, age can bring but gain
      Where Love goes always on before
And you walk with me in its train,
      Whom I will love for ever more.

Around us, when we first were wed,
  Keen were the winds that used to blow.
Now in our home, their garden-bed,
  The flowers of Love awake and grow:
Our children rise, our lives combine.
They are God's loveliest, holiest sign –
  His voice beyond the hurricane.
    He has bound us with a golden chain;
      He has laid before us all His store,
    That your delight may never wane,
      Whom I will love for ever more.

Because we love, we will not dread
  Days that are dark, or hopes brought low,
For by our faith we shall be fed.
  Our cup of joy shall spill, shall flow,
Yet still renew its draught of wine.
We need not fear the sun's decline,
  When night comes striding on amain;
    Sorrow we well may entertain;
      For God will teach us all the lore
    Of Heavenly Love – in you made plain,
      Whom I will love for ever more.

ENVOI

My Princess! Here, as to a shrine,
I bring my tribute, line by line,
  And here I end my artless strain.
    Oh! that my words were golden grain
      To give to you whom I adore –
    My wife, for whom my heart is fain,
      Whom I will love for ever more!

TO MUMMY WITH LOVE FROM FATHER CHRISTMAS

(HER PRESENT BEING DISGUISED AS RUDOLPH THE RED-NOSED REINDEER)

Long, long ago, on Christmas Morn,
Was little baby Jesus born,
And Eastern kings from far away
Came with their gifts to where He lay;
So every year my gifts I bear
To little children everywhere.

But it is Mummy, after all,
Who really makes our Festival.
Had she not struggled to prepare
And bake and buy with loving care
I should have travelled through the night
But found no happy home in sight –
No home to fill with children's mirth
In honour of the Baby's birth
Who is the King of all the earth.

So now it's Mummy's turn to meet
An unexpected Christmas treat;
And Rudolph comes on my behalf
He knows the way to make you laugh;
He knows – far more than you'd suppose,
Judging him by his funny nose –
And in his simple way reveals
The love that Father Christmas feels.

THESE FOOLISH THINGS

From obsessive contemplation
Of the faults, the irritation,
The affronts, the indignation
   Their embittered lives provoke
Cynics draw the sad conclusion
That delight is all delusion;
In concern they find confusion
   And in gentleness a joke.

But, instead of just despairing,
Let us do some more comparing;
For, in fact, we may be faring
   Rather better than they think.
When you hear the cynic hissing,
Sure it's just because he's missing
The companionship, the kissing,
   And the dancing and the drink.

Och! I know that self-denial
Is a form of earthly trial
Strongly recommended by all
   Who aspire to angels' wings.
Leave the saints to *that* endeavour.
Let the cynical be clever!
May our folly be for ever
   To enjoy these foolish things!

TO MISTRESS MARGARET THATCHER, 1989

Whither art tripping, Mistress Margaret?
Are not the Pinnacles of Power enough,
With even thy staunchest henchmen out of puff
And civil servants nervous and upset?
'Tis true thou hast not conquered Europe – yet;
But if thou shouldst decide to play it rough
There's not a man in Europe half as tough –
And that, forsooth, includes the Soviet!

There was a warrior maiden once in France
Who scourged the English, at the cost of burning!
"God and St Denis!" was her battle-cry.
But now it is the English who advance
And, with another Denis standing by,
Proclaim another lady "Not for turning!"

BALLADE

The Princess weeps in her lonely tower.
Her noble nose and her royal eye
Drip like leaves in an April shower
Till never a handkerchief hath she dry.
"Why hath he done this? Why, oh why
Hath he crushed my heart in his heartless fist
And filled my dreams with his faithless lie:
'Dear lips that quiver – you shall be kissed!'?"

How should she know, in her lofty bower,
What deadly dangers he must defy?
No treacherous varlet he, to cower,
But a strong man ready to do or die;
One who would never his love deny
Or falter in keeping his lady's tryst
(With its whispered password and soft reply:
"Dear lips that quiver!" – "You shall be kissed!").

So it doth not matter if storm-clouds lour,
If the way is long and the tower is high –
For his love is an overwhelming power!
If he needeth a pair of wings to fly
He can pluck an archangel right out of the sky!
(A poor old seraph could not resist.)
Then, plumed with light, see him turn and cry,
"Dear lips that quiver – you shall be kissed!"

ENVOI

Prithee, my Princess, do not sigh! –
Truthfully – out of the morning mist
He shall come to thee by and by.
Dear lips that quiver – you shall be kissed!

ANNIE DOWDLE

The long sea-lough of sleeping Carlingford –
What marvellous stories could its waves record!
For still, like jetsam stranded on the beach
Beyond the limits of the tidal reach,
Mysterious shapes and random hints remain.
Not all the past has been endured in vain.
In phrases and in legends linger on
Stray moments rescued from oblivion.

My home was in a cottage by the shore.
In winter storms I heard the breakers roar,
In summer played my childish games beside
The gentle rise and ebbing of the tide.
But even in a romantic place like this
Life is not always 'tragedy or bliss'.
Reality abhors the picturesque,
Preferring the absurd and the grotesque –
And what more crazy vision could there be
Than Annie Dowdle rising from the sea!

Nobody knows what made her, once a year,
Plunge, fully clothed, into the water there;
For in her months of wandering, in between,
Annie was not conspicuously clean.
Squealing with joy, she let her billowing skirt
Discharge its complement of fleas and dirt.
Her tattered blouse no washing could restore
But it was much, much cleaner than before.
What happened to her sticky underclothes
Must have been good – but Goodness only knows!
Only her silver hair, that drifted free
Among the silver bubbles of the sea,
Gave, somehow, to her annual pilgrimage
A touch of the serenity of age.

At last, when splashing could achieve no more,
Little old Annie Dowdle came ashore.
Her squelching boots left puddles everywhere,
But pride was in her step when, head in air,
As she had done for many a year before,
She made her way up to our cottage door.

She rang the bell, and when the housemaid came
She gave, not "Annie Dowdle" as her name,
But "Princess Annie". Dignified, exalted –
Nothing in her demeanour could be faulted.
What matter that she lacked a coronet
And that her royal robes were dripping wet!
Each year our cook and housemaid heard the tale
Of Princess Annie. Never did it fail
To bring conviction to their tender hearts.

It was a tale of Irish kings, that starts
In royal Tara, centuries ago,
Before the English came to overthrow
The ancient Royal House; a tale of flight
And royal children wandering through the night,
Homeless and penniless, until at last
Their lot amongst the tinkerfolk was cast;
A tale of how the line of kings kept on,
With all its rights and recognition gone,
Till now, when Princess Annie stood alone,
The last true claimant to the Irish throne.

There in our porch the Princess sat. Indoors
They could not let her come – and wet the floors;
But they brought out to her the silver tray,
The silver teapot, muffled in its gay
Embroidered cosy, and the silver jug
(Once, also, I believe, my christening mug);
And scones and cakes, served on my mother's best
Expensive china, for the royal guest.

At last, when Princess Annie had 'partaken',
She held her hand out (to be kissed, not shaken)
And blessed our house, and went upon her way
With squelching boots. And I can truly say
We never lost one spoon up Annie's sleeve –
A royal Princess would not stoop to thieve!

One day, my mother, for a moment stopping
Outside the grocer's, where she had been shopping,
Noticed a hearse with two black horses go
Cloppeting past her, reverent and slow.
There were no flowers – a pauper's funeral –
And not a single mourner there at all;
But hats were doffed, and all the people knew,
In the wee village, whom they doffed them to:
"Old Annie Dowdle – may God rest her soul!"
And in the church the bell began to toll.

Think you this bleak departure brought distress
To the proud spirit of the old Princess?
Not so – for all the angels clustered round
When Princess Annie heard the trumpets sound.

A WEDDING IN THE FAMILY

A wedding is a time for feeling glad
    (Though 'feeling glad' doesn't mean 'free from care' –
We ought to spare a thought for Mum and Dad!).

The youngest guests, of course, are going mad,
    Proclaiming – still with energy to spare! –
A wedding is a time for feeling glad.

Youthful high spirits shouldn't count as 'bad!'
    But Pandemonium just isn't fair!
We *ought* to spare a thought for Mum and Dad!

We've asked one guest I wish we never had;
    Offensive jokes like his pollute the air –
A wedding is a time for feeling *glad*.

Weddings are holy; this was no charade.
    Faith has been plighted by our bridal pair.
We ought to spare a thought for Mum and Dad

Who hope and fear, watching their lass – or lad –
    Step forward from the life they used to share.
A wedding is a time for feeling glad;
We ought to spare a thought for Mum and Dad.

AN AUTUMN WEDDING

Is there a sadness in an autumn wedding,
　When youth, with all its might-have-beens, has gone?
　Light-hearted paths in spring run on and on.
Youth does not heed the mountains it is treading;
It sees a boundless world beyond it spreading,
　With distant lands yet to be gazed upon.
　In autumn, guided by a misty sun,
Our tread is on the leaves the trees are shedding.

Yet love can turn to spring an autumn day
　For those who marry in their autumn-time.
　　Not saddened, but contented, hand-in-hand,
Why should they care how long or short the way?
　Still are there streams to cross and hills to climb
　　Before they gaze upon a distant land.

SONNET

Darkness, that in the moonlight magnifies
 The strange, transfigured shapes of normal day –
 Will there be only darkness left, to play
Its empty tricks when I have closed mine eyes?
No other sun, no other moon to rise;
 Darkness so deep that shadows melt away?
 Was it for this that we were young and gay
And that the mellowing years have made us wise?

We have no proof. We know that Christ was born,
 And lived, and was betrayed and crucified
 And in the silent darkness sepulchred...
 Nor need we proof that it was God who died;
That it was Truth who held the grave in scorn
 And turns our darkness to His living Word.

CREDO

i

The sun still gleams upon our ancient spires,
The ancient bells still consecrate the day;
But in the homes of men the ancient fires
Of certain faith sink low and die away.
Happy indeed were those who knelt to pray
Around a hearth which warmed them with its flame,
Where now the shadows gather, cold and grey!
Our God is dead; and nothing is the same;
With unbelieving hearts we mourn a vanished Name.

ii

What hope remains to cheer our orphaned lives?
Surely, like those who mourn, we fail to see
Beyond the dead the comfort that survives
Even in the dust of our mortality;
For dust itself is steeped in mystery.
Since out of nothing nothing can be made,
All that exists must trace its ancestry
From some First Cause, concealed and overlaid
By earth's forgotten past and childish dreams that fade.

iii

Mysterious dust! Dust that conforms to laws
No gods have made! Without intelligence,
Yet moulded with a skill that overawes
In its complexity our groping sense!
We see the function, not the Providence;
The world, we say, is cruel, meaningless...
Of all our fables, is the last pretence
To turn away our eyes in our distress
From the Creative Purpose that the stars confess?

iv

Not all the ages of expended time
Could have sufficed to marshal, one by one,
Fortuitous changes from primaeval slime
To this rich planet that we dwell upon.
Only Creative Purpose could have spun
Its robe of life over so young an Earth.
Not chance, but Evolution, sweeps us on,
Where human count of time has little worth;
Judged by the stars, our planet is of recent birth.

v

Earth holds its course through some dynamic plan;
And some great Intellect must lie behind
The sure progression leading up to Man,
However cruel, motiveless and blind,
The operation of its Laws we find.
Has human thought soared to some new dimension,
To sit in judgment on Creative Mind?
Or should we humbly search for the intention
Conceived by wisdom greater than our comprehension?

vi

Many would deem the search a foolish quest,
Fearing to launch conjecture on the swell
Beyond the waters we have charted best,
The laws we have observed and can foretell.
The Laws of Nature are immutable;
By prayers untouched, by no enchantment stirred;
No pity moves, nor chance, nor miracle
If some great Mind we look for, undeterred,
It is within unbroken laws the Voice is heard.

vii

The Laws of Nature, as we see them now,
Form one elaborate tableau, grouped and spaced;
Yet each has made its separate entrance bow,
And each the centre of the stage has graced,
And stepped aside, to be more humbly placed.

When fierce, tempestuous radioactivity
Comprised this Earth? What foresight could have traced
Its physics, or its laws of chemistry? –
Yet now each stands in place, unmoved perpetually.

viii

So that, when new-formed life in the ocean played
And drank primaeval protein to the lees
The Laws of Matter were already made.
Inanimate hazards of the stormy seas
Bruised and destroyed its cells; and, worse than these –
Since all Earth's protein had become alive –
Life preyed on life for Life's necessities.
The Laws of Life were fashioned: to survive,
Its tenuous cells must kill, and multiply, and strive.

ix

The moment came but once – and it was taken –
For Life to spring, however dread the price.
Matched with the silence of a world forsaken
Should we count Death a needless sacrifice?
If there seems cruelty in the device,
Tell me – what else did circumstance permit?
For fabled pumpkin and attendant mice
A magic wand is a solution fit;
But Reason found this way, and Life has followed it.

x

We cannot draw near this mysterious Mind
By musing on those early days alone.
We must contrast them with today to find,
In terms of change, the Purpose partly grown;
And, most of all, in Man will this be shown;
Man, who is born a mammal, and is fraught
With all the instincts that his kind have known;
And yet, within, how great a change is wrought!
Life dwells within the kingdom of self-conscious Thought.

xi

Knowledge, imagination – gradually
A strange new light flows over every sense;
And, of our instincts, it is Love we see
Become more human, growing more intense
As forms of life acquire intelligence.
No more, at first, than the desire to mate,
It rises, through possession and defence,
To that great unity of heart and fate
In selfless love which only death can separate.

xii

Love is a theme which has outsoared the voice
Of poets and of seers the ages long.
All we who love, and in its power rejoice,
Have caught at times the music of that song
Which from Eternal Truth is surely sprung.
This is the Numinous, by which we know –
With certainty which all the doubts that throng
Our restless minds can never overthrow –
That by this Truth we live and to this Truth we go.

xiii

The great evolving world in which we live
Within Creation's plan is still contained;
And none can give what is not his to give.
Our human minds can only be explained
As the endowment of a Mind which deigned
To share its power of thought with humankind.
And Love? – how should we dream it has remained
Unknown and unforeseen by such a Mind?
Surely the very source of Love is here enshrined!

xiv

That source of Love must be a Power which loves,
Just as the source of Wisdom must be wise.
Is not this God? – no tyrant king that moves
In arbitrary terror through the skies,
But still a Person, with a father's eyes.

When all the panoply of faith is shed
It is not God who falls, but His disguise.
The God of Love, whom we have mourned as dead,
Is still of all that lives the living fountainhead.

xv

Yet when we speak to Him He does not speak;
Nor does He warn when there is danger near.
This God of ours is One who does not break
The laws of His Creation, nor appear
In miracle, to answer hope or fear.
God does not rule, or warn, or shout us down.
Out of His dust evolved, we meet Him here,
Beneath whose Will our wills could not have grown;
For God to love our Selves they must remain our own.

xvi

Within our minds there is a compass, turned
Along the path which leads to what is true;
And God has waited there to be discerned
While seers and prophets added clue on clue,
And human understanding slowly grew,
Until in Christ Truth was a shining light.
With numinous completeness, Jesus knew;
The dove of Truth flew down and blessed His sight,
Filling His human spirit with the Infinite.

xvii

O God of Truth, by whom the world was made;
Whose unimaginable Love we see
For ever on the Cross of Christ portrayed,
Transforming Death to its Eternity;
Strengthen our human hands, that they may be
Throughout the world Love's ministers of Grace,
Until at last, and everlastingly,
All life shall find in Love its dwelling-place
And we shall meet our great Creator face to face.

POEMS

BY

PIERRE DE RONSARD

(1524 - 85)

AMOURS DE CASSANDRE

AMOURS DE MARIE

SONNETS POUR HÉLÈNE

TRANSLATED BY G. HASLETT CONNOR

TRANSLATIONS FROM PIERRE DE RONSARD

CONTENTS BY FIRST LINES

AMOURS DE CASSANDRE

AMOURS DE MARIE

SONNETS POUR HÉLÈNE

TRANSLATIONS FROM VARIOUS POETS

CONTENTS BY FIRST LINES

PIERRE DE RONSARD (1524 - 85)

Pierre de Ronsard was both a courtier and a courtier's son. After serving as a page to the Dauphin and to the royal Duke of Orléans he accompanied Princess Madeleine of France to Scotland for her wedding to the Scottish king. But the young Queen died, and he returned to France. A diplomatic career was cut short by deafness; instead, he became an eminent classical scholar. He supervised the education of the young King Charles IX and thereafter became his Court Poet. He was the foremost French lyric poet of his day, and is credited with establishing the Petrarchan Sonnet in French literature.

AMOURS DE CASSANDRE

These sonnets were written while Ronsard was in his twenties. Cassandre Salviati was a proud and sophisticated aristocrat. She was evidently not impressed by the posturing and 'broken heart' of a young poet over-full of paradoxes and classical allusions; and for Ronsard, one suspects, she represented an opportunity to perfect his poetic technique. When the affair ended it was his pride which suffered, rather than his heart.

AMOURS DE MARIE

On the rebound from Cassandre, Ronsard really did fall in love – with Marie Du Pin. There was nothing aristocratic about Marie. She was a simple, practical girl, with no literary interests. Ronsard had to cut out all the frills from his style, which greatly improved it. He was more relaxed; these poems were written 'for fun'; they bubble over with playful tenderness. Yet all the while his mastery of the Petrarchan sonnet was growing more assured. But Marie died. The formal language of his last two sonnets for her throbs with genuine grief.

SONNETS POUR HÉLÈNE

These sonnets were written about twenty-five years later – for Hélène de Surgères. Hélène may initially have been flattered by the attentions of a famous poet, but she was a maid of honour to Catherine de Medici, and too level-headed to become deeply involved with a suitor old enough to be her father. "Sonnets Pour Hélène" end with the death of Ronsard's royal patron, Charles IX. This group of sonnets is considered to be Ronsard's masterpiece. Several English poets, including Yeats, have been 'inspired' by the sonnet "Quand vous serez bien vieille, au soir, à la chandelle…"

TRANSLATIONS FROM RONSARD'S 'AMOURS DE CASSANDRE'

Je vous envoie un bouquet que ma main
   Vient de trier de ces fleurs épanies
   Qui ne les eust à ce vespre cueuillies
Cheutes à terre elles fussent demain.
Cela vous soit un exemple certain
   Que vos beautez, bien qu'elles soient fleuries,
   En peu de temps cherront toutes fletries,
Et, comme fleurs, periront tout soudain.

Le temps s'en va, le temps s'en va, ma dame.
   Las! le temps non, mais nous, nous en allons
Et tost serons estendus sous la lame;
   Et des amours desquelles nous parlons
      Quand serons morts ne sera plus nouvelle;
      Pour ce, aymez-moy, ce pendant qu'estes belle.

TRANSLATION

I am sending you a posy that my hand
    Has picked where here the flowers are blossoming –
    Which, had they not been picked this evening,
Tomorrow would be scattered o'er the land.
May this as an example for you stand
    That these your charms, though ne'er so flourishing,
    Must in a little while be withering
And then, like flowers, suddenly disband.

Time passes on, my lady, passes on;
    Ah no! Not Time, but we – 'tis we who pass
And soon shall lie outstretched beneath the lawn.
    And of the loves we talk of now – alas!
        When we are dead no rumour shall be there;
        Then love, Oh love me, while you still are fair!

TRANSLATIONS FROM RONSARD'S 'AMOURS DE CASSANDRE'

Mignonne, allons voir si la rose
Qui ce matin avait déclose
   Sa robe de pourpre au Soleil,
A point perdu cette véprée
Les plis de sa robe pourprée
   Et son teint au vôtre pareil.

Las! Voyez comme en peu d'espace,
Mignonne, elle a dessus la place,
   Las! las! ses beautés laissé choir!
O vraiment marâtre Nature,
Puisqu'une telle fleur ne dure
   Que du matin jusques au soir!

Donc, si vous me croyez, mignonne,
Tandis que votre âge fleuronne
   En sa plus verte nouveauté,
Cueillez, cueillez votre jeunesse:
Comme à cette fleur la vieillesse
   Fera ternir votre beauté.

TRANSLATION

Come, my sweet, and see the rose
That, today, her royal clothes
   To the rising sun hath shown.
Now, as twilight falls, are shed
All her draperies, and fled
   Colours rivalling your own.

See, alas! how soon, my sweet,
All her beauties, in defeat,
   Now lie scattered far and wide.
Cruel Nature! – thus to give
Such a flower a span to live
   But from morn till eventide!

Sweet, believe me when I say:
While your youth is on display,
   Fresh and green and newly-made,
Gather, treasure and enjoy!
Age, that could this flower destroy,
   Soon will make your beauty fade.

TRANSLATIONS FROM RONSARD'S 'AMOURS DE CASSANDRE'

J'espère et crains, je me tais et supplie
   Or' je suis glace, et ores un feu chaud,
   J'admire tout, et de rien ne me chaut,
Je me délace, et mon col je relie.
Rien ne me plaît, sinon ce qui m'ennuie,
   Je suis vaillant, et le coeur me défaut,
   J'ai l'espoir bas, j'ai le courage haut,
Je doute Amour et si je le défie.

Plus je me pique, et plus je suis rétif,
J'aime être libre, et veux être captif,
   Tout je désire, et si n'ai qu'une envie.
   Un Prométhée en passions je suis:
   J'ose, je veux, je m'efforce, et ne puis,
Tant d'un fil noir la Parque ourdit ma vie.

TRANSLATION

I hope, I fear, keep silent or complain,
By turns as cold as ice, as hot as fire.
All kinds of things – or nothing – I admire
(Even my necktie is untied again!).
I care for only what I most disdain;
When my heart sinks my courage rises higher;
When hope is low, then do I most aspire –
Dreading the Love I scorn to entertain!

I spur myself by digging in my heels!
Freedom I love, yet servitude appeals,
And boundless hopes are just one hope for me.
My passions blaze on a Promethean scale:
I wish, I dare, I strive – to no avail,
For Fate's black thread has warped my destiny!

TRANSLATIONS FROM RONSARD'S 'AMOURS DE CASSANDRE'

Amour me tue, et si je ne veux dire
  Le plaisant mal que ce m'est de mourir,
  Tant j'ai grand peur qu'on veuille secourir
Le doux tourment pour lequel je soupire.
Il est bien vrai que ma langueur désire
  Qu'avec le temps je me puisse guérir,
  Mais je ne veux ma dame requérir
Pour ma santé, tant me plaît mon martyre.

Tais-toi, langueur, je sens venir le jour
Que ma maîtresse, après si long séjour,
  Voyant le mal que son orgueil me donne,
    Qu'à la douceur la rigueur fera lieu,
    En imitant la nature de Dieu
Qui nous tourmente, et puis il nous pardonne.

TRANSLATION

Though love is killing me, I must not say
   How pleasurable such a death can be.
   Someone, I fear, may try to rescue me
From the sweet agony for which I pray!
Yes! It is true that I would hope some day
   From my love-sickness to be wholly free;
   But to my lady I would make no plea
To take this pleasing martyrdom away.

Courage, faint heart! After so many days
That day is coming when my mistress' gaze
   Shall see the suffering her pride has sent.
      Then shall her scorn be turned to sweet accord,
     In keeping with the nature of our Lord
Who grants us pardon after punishment.

TRANSLATIONS FROM RONSARD'S 'AMOURS DE CASSANDRE'

Comme un chevreuil, quand le printemps détruit
Du froid hiver la poignante gelée,
Pour mieux brouter la feuille emmiellée,
Hors de son bois avec l'aube s'en fuit;
Et seul et sûr, loin de chiens et de bruit,
Or' sur un mont, or' dans une vallée,
Or' près d'une onde à l'écart recelée,
Libre, folâtre où son pied le conduit;

De rets ni d'arc sa liberté n'a crainte,
Sinon alors que sa vie est atteinte
D'un trait meurtrier empourpré de son sang;
Ainsi j'allais sans espoir de dommage
Le jour qu'un oeil, sur l'avril de mon âge,
Tira d'un coup mille traits en mon flanc.

TRANSLATION

The young roe deer, whom early spring has freed
　From the keen frost of cold and wintry days,
　In search of tender leaves on which to graze
Ventures at daybreak from his wood, to feed.
Alone (there are no barking dogs to heed),
　Over the hill or down the glen he strays
　Till the sea's curling breakers he surveys
And idly wanders where his foot may lead.

His freedom reckons not with trap or bow
Until his life is suddenly brought low –
　With his red blood the murderous arrow's stained...
　　I, too, was blithely wandering, free of fears,
　　When that one glance, in the April of my years,
　Into my side a thousand arrows rained.

TRANSLATIONS FROM RONSARD'S 'AMOURS DE CASSANDRE'

Heureux le jour, l'an, le mois et la place,
    L'heure et le temps où vos yeux m'ont tué,
    Sinon tué, à tout le moins mué,
Comme Méduse, en une froide glace.
Il est bien vrai que le trait de ma face
    Me reste encor, mais l'esprit délié
    Pour vivre en vous, a son corps oublié,
Me laissant seul, comme une froide masse.

Aucunefois, quand vous tournez un peu
Vos yeux sur moi, je sens un petit feu
    Qui me ranime, et réchauffe les veines,
      Et fait au froid quelque petit effort.
    Mais vos regards n'allongent que mes peines,
      Tant le premier fut cause de ma mort!

TRANSLATION

Happy the day, the year, the month, the place,
   The moment when your bright eyes struck me dead!
   Or, if not dead, at least immured instead,
A captive in Medusa's icy case.
I know it's true that outwardly my face
   Remains unaltered, but my soul has fled
   To live in you, its cast-off body shed
Like a lump of ice, alone and in disgrace.

From time to time, when you have turned your gaze
Briefly upon me, I have felt a blaze
   Bring me to life and heat my frozen veins,
      Making cold sinews twitch in one more try.
   Your glances, though, can but prolong my pains –
      It was the first of them that made me die!

TRANSLATIONS FROM RONSARD'S 'AMOURS DE CASSANDRE'

Je parangonne à ta jeune beauté
 Qui toujours dure, en son printemps nouvelle,
 Ce mois d'avril, qui ses fleurs renouvelle
En sa plus gaie et verte nouveauté.
Loin devant toi fuira la cruauté,
 Devant lui fuit la saison plus cruelle;
 Il est tout beau, ta face est toute belle;
Ferme est son cours, ferme est ta loyauté.

Il peint les bords, les forêts et les plaines,
 Tu peins mes vers d'un bel émail de fleurs;
Des laboureurs il arrose les peines,
 D'un vain espoir tu laves mes douleurs;
 Du ciel sur l'herbe il fait tomber les pleurs,
Tu fais sortir de mes yeux deux fontaines.

TRANSLATION

I hold thy youthful loveliness to be,
　In the unfaltering freshness of thy spring,
　Like April, when the flowers are burgeoning,
Rejoicing in their new-found greenery.
Far from thy path all cruelty shall flee,
　As winter's cruel months have taken wing;
　Now April blooms, as thou art blossoming;
It holds its course, thou thine integrity.

Woodlands and plains it paints and glorifies;
　My verse thy beauty, like a flower, inspires.
The labourer's back is wet by April skies;
　My grief thou hast washed clear of vain desires.
　In April, tears from heaven the land requires;
Thou hast made fountains of my weeping eyes.

TRANSLATIONS FROM RONSARD'S 'AMOURS DE CASSANDRE'

Je veux brûler, pour m'emvoler aux cieux,
  Tout l'imparfait de mon écorce humaine,
  M'éternisant comme le fils d'Alcmène,
Qui tout en feu s'assit entre les dieux.
Jà mon esprit, désireux de son mieux
  Dedans ma chair, rebelle, se promène,
  Et jà le bois de sa victime amène
Pour s'immoler aux rayons de tes yeux.

O saint brasier, ô flamme entretenue
  D'un feu divin, advienne que ton chaud
Brûle si bien ma dépouille connue,
  Que, libre et nu, je vole d'un plein saut
  Outre le ciel, pour adorer là-haut
L'autre beauté dont la tienne est venue!

TRANSLATION

Oh let me burn – that I may reach the skies –
All imperfections from my human frame!
As rose Alcmena's son when, wrapped in flame,
He found amongst the gods his deathless prize.
Within my soul such aspirations rise
As my weak flesh can neither hold nor tame;
My faggots wait to burn me and proclaim
Through sacrifice the brightness of thine eyes.

O sacred pyre! O flame descended from
A fire divine! Do not thy heat deny,
But let it my discarded self consume.
Naked and free, let me leap up and fly
Beyond the aether, to adore on high
That other beauty from which thine hath come!

TRANSLATIONS FROM RONSARD'S 'AMOURS DE CASSANDRE'

Ciel, air et vents, plains et monts découverts,
Tertres vineux et forêts verdoyantes,
Rivages torts et sources ondoyantes,
Taillis rasés et vous bocages verts,
Antres moussus à demi-front ouverts,
Près, boutons, fleurs et herbes roussoyantes,
Vallons bossus et plages blondoyantes,
Et vous rochers, les hôtes de mes vers,

Puis qu'au partir, rongé de soin et d'ire,
A ce bel oeil Adieu je n'ai su dire,
Qui près et loin me détient en émoi,
Je vous supplie, ciel, air, vents, monts et plaines,
Taillis, forêts, rivages et fontaines,
Antres, près, fleurs, dites-le-lui pour moi.

TRANSLATION

Sky, air, winds, plains, crags where no verdure stays,
  Vine-covered slopes and forests flourishing!
  Ye winding banks, and every rippling spring!
Trim copses, too, and leafy woodland ways!
Caverns, moss-browed, with half-averted gaze!
  And meadows and flowers and grasses ripening!
  Hear, golden strands, and glens meandering,
And rocks – all celebrated in my lays!...

Though we must part, though pain and anger swell,
How can I bid those lovely eyes farewell
  That, near or far, still claim my fealty?
    I beg you, sky, air, winds and plains and mountains,
    Copses and forests, river banks and fountains,
Caves, meadows, flowers – tell them so for me!

TRANSLATIONS FROM RONSARD'S 'AMOURS DE CASSANDRE'

Je veux lire en trois jours l'*Iliade* d'Homère
    Et pour ce, Corydon, ferme bien l'huis sur moi;
    Si rien me vient troubler, je t'assure, ma foi,
Tu sentiras combien pesante est ma colère.
Je ne veux seulement que notre chambrière
    Vienne faire mon lit, ton compagnon, ni toi.
    Je veux trois jours entiers demeurer à recoi,
Pour folâtrer après une semaine entière.

Mais si quelqu'un venait de la part de Cassandre,
Ouvre-lui tôt la porte, et ne le fais attendre,
    Soudain entre en ma chambre et me viens accoutrer.
    Je veux tant seulement à lui seul me montrer;
Au reste, si un dieu voulait pour moi descendre
    Du ciel, ferme la porte et ne le laisse entrer.

TRANSLATION

Three days to read through Homer's *Iliad*!
   So, Corydon, be off, and shut the door!
   If I am interrupted any more,
By Heavens! I'll teach you not to make me mad!
The house-boy will be all I'll need, my lad;
   Making my bed you won't be needed for.
   I want three days of quiet, to restore
My jangled nerves after the week I've had!

But if Cassandra sends a messenger
Open at once! Don't keep him waiting here.
   Come straight into my room and get me dressed –
   Though he would be my only welcome guest;
Even if a god should down from Heaven appear
   To see me – shut him out with all the rest!

TRANSLATIONS FROM RONSARD'S 'AMOURS DE MARIE'

Marie, qui voudrait votre nom retourner,
  Il trouverait: AIMER; aimez-moi donc, Marie.
  Votre nom de nature à l'amour vous convie.
A qui trahit Nature, il ne faut pardonner.
S'il vous plaît votre coeur pour gage me donner,
  Je vous offre le mien; ainsi de cette vie
  Nous prendrons les plaisirs, et jamais autre envie
Ne me pourra l'esprit d'une autre emprisonner.

Il faut aimer, maîtresse, au monde quelque chose.
Celui qui n'aime point, malheureux se propose
  Une vie d'un Scythe, et ses jours veut passer
  Sans goûter la douceur des douceurs la meilleure.
Rien n'est doux sans Vénus et sans son fils: à l'heure
  Que je n'aimerai plus, puisse-je trépasser!

TRANSLATION

Marie, since he who would transpose your name
    Would find: AIMER – to love – love me, Marie!
    Love and your name by nature should agree;
And to deny our nature is a shame!
Were you to pledge your heart, with love aflame,
    Then would I pledge you mine as faithfully,
    And all life's joys would come to you and me;
No other soul but yours my heart would claim.

On earth we must love something, lady mine.
He who loves naught does for himself design
      A wretched, Scythian life. His days go by,
    But the sweetest thing of all he has not tasted:
Life without Venus and her son is wasted.
    When I have ceased to love then let me die.

TRANSLATIONS FROM RONSARD'S 'AMOURS DE MARIE'

LA QUENOUILLE – THE DISTAFF

Quenouille, de Pallas la compagne et l'amie,
Cher présent que je porte à ma chère Marie,
Afin de soulager l'ennui qu'elle a de moi,
Disant quelque chanson en filant dessus toi,
Faisant pirouetter à son huis, amusée,
Tout le jour son rouet et sa grosse fusée.

Quenouille, je te mène où je suis arrêté;
Je voudrais racheter par toi ma liberté.
Tu ne viendras ès mains d'une mignonne oisive
Qui ne fait qu'attiser sa perruque lascive
Et qui perd tout son temps à mirer et farder
Sa face, à celle fin qu'on l'aille regarder,
Mais bien entre les mains d'une disposte fille
Qui dévide, qui coud, qui ménage et qui file
Avecques ses deux soeurs pour tromper ses ennuis
L'hiver devant le feu, l'été devant son huis.

Aussi je ne voudrais que toi, quenouille, faite
En notre Vendômois (où le peuple regrette
Le jour qui passe en vain), allasses en Anjou
Pour demeurer oisive et te rouiller au clou.
Je te puis assurer que sa main délicate
Filera dextrement quelque drap d'écarlate,
Qui si fin et si souëf en sa laine sera
Que pour un jour de fête un roi le vêtira.

TRANSLATION

O Distaff! – to Pallas, companion and friend!
Dear present that I for dear Marie intend!
To make up for the boredom she tells me I bring
May she take you in hand and light-heartedly sing,
While her spinning wheel busily spins at her door
All day, in great spindlefuls – more and yet more!

You are sharing my banishment, distaff, with me,
For I hope that through you I may soon be set free.
No lazy coquette will possess you, for sure,
Who does nothing but pat her seductive coiffure
And who endlessly alters her painted complexion
In hope that the world will admire its perfection.
A wide-awake girl's are the hands *you*'ll be in!
She can sew and keep house, she can wind, she can spin,
With two sisters to lighten her labours, before
In the winter her hearth, and in summer her door.

What I choose for you, distaff, is only the best.
We are both from Vendôme (where the people protest
If they've wasted one day!); I would not have you trail
All the way to Anjou just to rust on a nail!
Your new mistress – believe me! – her touch is so neat
That if some scarlet cloth she should choose to complete
In such delicate folds would the drapery fall
That a king might well choose it to wear at a ball.

Suis-moi donc, tu seras la plus que bienvenue,
Quenouille, des deux bouts et grêlette et menue,
Un peu grosse au milieu, où la filasse tient,
Etreinte d'un ruban qui de Montoire vient.
Aime-laine, aime-fil, aime-étaim, maisonnière,
Longue, Palladienne, enflée, chansonnière,
Suis-moi, laisse Couture et allons à Bourgueil,
Où, quenouille, on te doit recevoir d'un bon oeil,
Car le petit présent qu'un loyal ami donne
Passe des puissants rois le sceptre et la couronne.

So – come with me, distaff! You'll soon be with friends,
Displaying your slender and tapering ends
(Rather plump round the middle, from holding the tow,
Where a fine Montoire ribbon is tied in a bow).
You love carding and wool; you love thread; you are long
In Palladian pride, yet at home in your song.
So be done with Couture! We'll be off to Bourgueil
Where, distaff, you ought to be welcomed with joy;
For though simple the present a true lover brings
It is more than the crown and the sceptre of kings.

TRANSLATIONS FROM RONSARD'S 'AMOURS DE MARIE'

CHANSON

Quand ce beau printemps je vois
  J'aperçois
Rajeunir la terre et l'onde,
Et me semble que le jour,
  Et l'amour,
Comme enfants naissent au monde.

Le jour, qui plus beau se fait,
  Nous refait
Plus belle et verte la terre,
Et Amour armé de traits
  Et d'attraits
En nos coeurs il fait la guerre.

Il répand de toutes parts
  Feux et dards
Et dompte sous sa puissance
Hommes, bêtes et oiseaux,
  Et les eaux
Lui rendent obéissance.

Vénus avec son enfant
  Triomphant
Au haut de son coche assise
Laisse ses cygnes voler
  Parmi l'air
Pour aller voir son Anchise.

SONG

When the sweet spring I see
  It seems to me
That youth returns to earth
And that the daylight, too,
  And love are new
As babies are at birth.

A day so glorious
  Creates for us
A land more green by far;
But Love, although he charms,
  With deadly arms
Upon our hearts makes war.

In earth's remotest parts
  His flaming darts
Proclaim his power complete.
Man, beast and bird bow low
  And waters flow
In homage at his feet.

Then Venus and her boy
  Are filled with joy
And in her chariot ride,
Bidding her swans to bear
  Them through the air
To her Anchises' side.

CHANSON (continué)

Quelque part que ses beaux yeux
 Par les cieux
Tournent leurs lumières belles
L'air, qui se montre serein,
 Est tout plein
D'amoureuses étincelles.

Puis, en descendant à bas,
 Sous ses pas,
Naissent mille fleurs écloses;
Les beaux lis et les oeillets
 Vermeillets
Rougissent entre les roses.

Je sens en ce mois si beau
 Le flambeau
D'Amour qui m'échauffe l'âme,
Y voyant de tous côtés
 Les beautés
Qu'il emprunte de ma dame.

Quand je vois tout de couleurs
 Et de fleurs
Qui émaillent un rivage,
Je pense voir le beau teint
 Qui est peint
Si vermeil en son visage.

Quand je vois les grands rameaux
 Des ormeaux
Qui sont lacés de lierre,
Je pense être pris ès lacs
 De ses bras,
Et que mon col elle serre.

SONG (continued)

Wherever her bright eyes,
  Piercing the skies,
Send forth their gleaming sight
The cool and tranquil air
  Is seen to flare
In love-lit points of light.

And when on earth below
  Her footsteps go
A thousand flowers expand.
There pinks and lilies vie
  Or blushingly
Among the roses stand.

This very month there came
  The golden flame
Of Love, to warm my heart,
Seeing that everywhere
  Her beauties rare
My lady doth impart.

Enamelled blossoms flank
  The river bank
And there I fain would seek
Those flowers in which their tint
  Is like a print
Made by her rosy cheek.

Great branches cannot free
  The young elm tree
When twining ivies tangle...
I feel her arms enfold,
  And then take hold –
I feel them squeeze and strangle!

CHANSON (continué)

Quand j'entends la douce voix
   Par les bois
Du gai rossignol qui chante,
D'elle je pense jouir
   Et ouïr
Sa douce voix qui m'enchante.

Quand je vois en quelque endroit
   Un pin droit,
Ou quelque arbre qui s'élève,
Je me laisse décevoir,
   Pensant voir
Sa belle taille est sa grève.

Quand je vois dans un jardin,
   Au matin,
S'éclore une fleur nouvelle,
J'accompare le bouton
   Au téton
De son beau sein qui pommelle.

Quand le soleil tout riant
   D'orient
Nous montre sa blonde tresse,
Il me semble que je voi
   Devant moi
Lever ma belle maîtresse.

Quand je sens parmi les prés
   Diaprés
Les fleurs dont la terre est pleine,
Lors je fais croire à mes sens
   Que je sens
La douceur de son haleine.

SONG (continued)

When in some forest glade
  Its serenade
Reveals the nightingale,
I hear – and I rejoice –
  My lady's voice
Holding me in its spell.

When some tall pine I see,
  Or other tree
Majestic in its place,
I let myself perceive
  In make-believe
Her tall and slender grace.

When at an early hour
  A garden flower
Is first made manifest,
To me the bud so neat
  Is like the teat
Upon her rounded breast.

When in the east the sun,
  Laughing in fun,
Shows us his golden hair,
It is as if I see
  In front of me
My mistress rising there.

When in the open field
  Lie unconcealed
The flowers of Nature, wreathing,
Then of my dame I think
  And long to drink
The fragrance of her breathing.

CHANSON (continué)

Bref, je fais comparaison
  Par raison
Du printemps et de m'amie:
Il donne aux fleurs la vigueur,
  Et mon coeur
D'elle prend vigueur et vie.

SONG (continued)

To such comparison
  Am I led on
By spring and by my dame.
In spring the flowers start;
  From her my heart
Receives its vital flame.

TRANSLATIONS FROM RONSARD'S 'AMOURS DE MARIE'

CHANSON

Le printemps n'a point de fleurs,
L'automne tant de raisins meurs,
L'été tant de chaleurs hâlées,
L'hiver tant de froides gelées,
Ni la mer n'a tant de poissons,
Ni la Beauce tant de moissons,
Ni la Bretagne tant d'arènes,
Ni l'Auvergne tant de fontaines,
Ni la nuit tant de clairs flambeaux,
Ni les forêts tant de rameaux
Que je porte au coeur, ma maîtresse,
Pour vous de peine et de tristesse.

SONG

More than all the flowers of spring,
Or grapes in autumn ripening,
More than summer's burning gold,
More than winter's icy cold,
More than fishes in the deep,
More harvest than in Beauce they reap,
More than the sand in Breton bays,
More fountains than Auvergne displays,
More than night is lit with flares,
More branches than the forest bears –

More than all these, my heart doth pine
For love of thee, O lady mine!

TRANSLATIONS FROM RONSARD'S 'AMOURS DE MARIE'

Marie, levez-vous, vous êtes paresseuse:
  Jà la gaie alouette au ciel a fredonné,
  Et jà le rossignol doucement jargonné,
Dessus l'épine assis, sa complainte amoureuse.
Sus! debout! allons voir l'herbelette perleuse,
  Et votre beau rosier de boutons coronné,
  Et vos oeillets mignons auxquels aviez donné,
Hier au soir, de l'eau, d'une main si soigneuse.

Harsoir en vous couchant vous jurates vos yeux
  D'etre plus tôt que moi ce matin éveillée;
Mais le dormir de l'Aube, aux filles gracieux,
  Vous tient d'un doux sommeil encor les yeux sillée.
    Ça! ça! que je les baise et votre beau tétin
    Cent fois, pour vous apprendre à vous lever matin.

TRANSLATION

Wake up, Marie – you little sleepyhead!
   The skylark's song has to the sky been borne,
   And now the nightingale upon the thorn
Falls silent, for love's sorrows are all said.
Come! Let us see the dewy mead, instead;
   And your sweet rose, which many buds adorn;
   And poppies, which no longer droop forlorn,
Saved by the water that your hand has shed.

You vowed, last night at bedtime, that your eyes
   Sooner than mine would greet the morning light,
But that full sleep at dawn which maidens prize
   In gentle slumber keeps your eyes shut tight!
      How gladly would I kiss them – and your breast –
      A hundred times, in bidding you be dressed!

TRANSLATIONS FROM RONSARD'S 'AMOURS DE MARIE'

Terre, ouvre-moi ton sein, et me laisse reprendre
  Mon trésor, que la Parque a caché dessous toi,
  Ou bien, si tu ne peux, ô terre, cache-moi
Sous même sépulture avec sa belle cendre.
La trait qui la tua devait faire descendre
  Mon corps auprès du sien, pour finir mon émoi;
  Aussi bien, vu le mal qu'en sa mort je reçois,
Je ne saurais plus vivre, et me fâche d'attendre.

Quand ses yeux m'éclairaient et qu'en terre j'avais
Le bonheur de les voir, à l'heure je vivais
  Ayant de leurs rayons mon âme gouvernée.
    Maintenant je suis mort: la Mort qui s'en alla
    Loger dedans ses yeux, en partant m'appela,
Et me fit de son soir accomplir ma journée.

TRANSLATION

Open thy bosom, earth! Let me again
    Enjoy the treasure that Fate hath buried there!
    Or, if thou canst not do so, let me share
The tomb which doth her lovely dust contain.
The arrow that hath killed her should have slain
    My body, too, and ended my despair.
    I know not how to live, or why, or where,
For she is dead and I am torn with pain.

When her eyes shone upon me, and earth could give
The joy of beholding them, then I did live!
    My very soul was governed by their ray.
        But now I, too, am dead; for when Death came
        And lodged within her eyes he called my name
And made me with their darkness end my day.

TRANSLATIONS FROM RONSARD'S 'AMOURS DE MARIE'

Comme on voit sur la branche, au mois de mai, la rose
En sa belle jeunesse, en sa première fleur,
Rendre le ciel jaloux de sa vive couleur,
Quand l'aube de ses pleurs, au point du jour, l'arrose;
La grâce dans sa feuille, et l'amour, se repose,
Embaumant les jardins et les arbres d'odeur,
Mais battue ou de pluie, ou d'excessive ardeur,
Languissante elle meurt, feuille à feuille déclose;

Ainsi, en ta première et jeune nouveauté,
Quand la terre et le ciel honoraient ta beauté,
La Parque t'a tuée, et cendre tu reposes.
Pour obsèques reçois mes larmes et mes pleurs,
Ce vase plein de lait, ce panier plein de fleurs,
Afin que vif et mort ton corps ne soit que roses.

TRANSLATION

The rose that blossoms on its stem in May
In all its promise, beautiful and new,
Makes the sky jealous of its vivid hue
When morning weeps on it at break of day.
Then grace and love within its petals stay
And with their fragrance all the glades imbue –
But should fierce rain or scorching heat ensue
The rose must die, its petals fall away.

You were as sweet, as beautiful, as young;
In heaven and on the earth your praise was sung
Until Fate struck, and dust reclaimed you, too.
With tears I bring you, from this world of ours,
A stoup of milk, a basket full of flowers,
For roses live, and roses die, with you.

TRANSLATIONS FROM RONSARD'S 'SONNETS POUR HÉLÈNE'

L'autre jour que j'étais sur le haut d'un degré,
    Passant, tu m'avisas, et me tournant la vue,
    Tu m'éblouis les yeux, tant j'avais l'âme émue
De me voir en sursaut de tes yeux rencontré.
Ton regard dans le coeur, dans le sang m'est entré
    Comme un éclat de foudre alors qu'il fend la nue;
    J'eus de froid et de chaud la fièvre continue,
D'un si poignant regard mortellement outré.

Lors si ta belle main passant ne m'eût fait signe,
Main blanche, qui se vante être fille d'un cygne,
    Je fusse mort, Hélène, aux rayons de tes yeux;
    Mais ton signe retint l'âme presque ravie.
Ton oeil se contenta d'être victorieux,
    Ta main se réjouit de me donner la vie.

TRANSLATION

I was standing upon a step the other day,
 When you passed by, and turned, and looked at me.
 It dazzled, it confused me utterly,
When your bright eyes first held me as their prey.
Into my heart and blood they sped their way
 Like lightning through a storm-cloud bursting free.
 Now hot, now cold, in feverish agony,
I felt so keen a glance would surely slay!

Then, as you passed, your fair hand gave a sign
(White, as if from a swan you traced your line!)...
 Oh, Helen! through your gaze I would have died!
 It was your gesture let my soul revive.
 Your eyes with victory were satisfied;
 Your hand rejoiced in saving me alive.

TRANSLATIONS FROM RONSARD'S 'SONNETS POUR HÉLÈNE'

Trois ans sont jà passés que ton oeil me tient pris,
　　Et si ne suis marri de me voir en servage;
　　Seulement je me deuls des ailes de mon âge,
Qui me laissent le chef semé de cheveux gris.
Si tu me vois où pâle, ou de fièvre surpris,
　　Quelquefois solitaire, ou triste de visage,
　　Tu devrais d'un regard soulager mon dommage:
L'Aurore ne met point son Tithon à mépris.

Si tu es de mon mal seule cause première,
　　Il faut que de mon mal tu sentes les effets:
C'est une sympathie aux hommes contumière.
　　Je suis (j'en jure Amour) tout tel que tu me fais;
Tu es mon coeur, mon sang, ma vie et ma lumière;
　　Seule je te choisis, seule aussi tu me plais.

TRANSLATION

Three years have passed since I was bound and sworn
  In service to your eyes – with no regret,
  Save that – alas! – the wings of age have let
A sprinkling of grey hairs my head adorn.
If you should see me pale, or fever-worn –
  My face at times in lonely sadness set –
  Give me one smile, and all my needs are met!
Aurora does not her Tithonus scorn.

Since you alone have brought me to this plight
  You must not turn aside, insensitive,
From those who claim your sympathy of right.
  All that I am, Love knows, is what you give.
You are my heart, my blood, my life, my light,
  My chosen one, for whom alone I live.

TRANSLATIONS FROM RONSARD'S 'SONNETS POUR HÉLÈNE'

Te regardant assise auprès de ta cousine,
  Belle comme une aurore, et toi comme un soleil,
  Je pensai voir deux fleurs d'un même teint pareil,
Croissantes en beauté, l'une à l'autre voisine.
La chaste, sainte, belle et unique Angevine,
  Vite comme un éclair, sur moi jeta son oeil;
  Toi, comme paresseuse et pleine de sommeil,
D'un seul petit regard tu ne m'estimas digne.

Tu t'entretenais seule, au visage abaissé,
  Pensive, toute à toi, n'aimant rien que toi-même,
Dédaignant à chacun d'un sourcil ramassé,
  Comme une qui ne veut qu'on la cherche où qu'on l'aime.
  J'eus peur de ton silence et m'en allai tout blême,
Craignant que mon salut n'eût ton oeil offensé.

TRANSLATION

Your sitting with your cousin set the scene!
   Fair as the dawn was she, as sunlight you!
   Methought I saw two blossoms of one hue
Growing in beauty, with no space between.
The pure, sweet, lovely, matchless Angevine
   Saw me like lightning as I came in view –
   But you to languid reverie withdrew,
As if to see me would your worth demean.

With downcast gaze, into your soul retreating,
   You asked no more than to be left alone –
All overtures with wrinkled brow defeating,
   And choosing to be friendless and unknown.
   I fled your silence, pale and fearful grown
That I might have offended you by greeting.

TRANSLATIONS FROM RONSARD'S 'SONNETS POUR HÉLÈNE'

Je liai d'un filet de soie cramoisie
  Votre bras l'autre jour, parlant avecques vous,
  Mais le bras seulement fut captif de mes nouds (noeuds)
Sans vous pouvoir lier ni coeur ni fantaisie.
Beauté, que pour maîtresse unique j'ai choisie,
  Le sort est inégal: vous triomphez de nous,
  Vous me tenez esclave, esprit, bras et genoux,
Et Amour ne vous tient ni prise ni saisie.

Je veux parler, maîtresse, à quelque vieil sorcier,
Afin qu'il puisse au mien votre vouloir lier,
  Et qu'une même plaie à nos coeurs soit semblable.
    Je faux: l'amour qu'on charme est de peu de séjour;
  Etre beau, jeune, riche, éloquent, agréable,
    Non les vers enchantés, sont les sorciers d'Amour.

TRANSLATION

I tied a thread of crimson silk around
  Your arm, while we were talking yesterday –
  Your arm, but nothing more. I cannot say
That round your dreaming heart my thread was wound.
My lady Beauty, whom I have sought and found,
  Unequal is our fate! Beneath your sway
  Captive in body and in soul I stay –
But Love has never captured you, nor bound.

With some old sorcerer would I conspire
To bind your dreams with mine in one desire
  Till our two heartbeats mingle, each with each.
      Fond hope! Enchanted loves too fleeting prove.
Youthful good looks, wealth, charm and honeyed speech –
  Not incantations – cast the spells of Love!

TRANSLATIONS FROM RONSARD'S 'SONNETS POUR HÉLÈNE'

Nous promenant tout seuls, vous me dîtes, maîtresse,
  Qu'un chant vous déplaisait s'il était doucereux,
  Que vous aimiez les plaints des tristes amoureux,
Tout voix lamentable et pleine de tristesse.
"Et pour ce (disiez vous), quand je suis loin de presse,
  Je choisis vos sonnets qui sont plus douloureux,
  Puis d'un chant qui est propre au sujet langoureux
Ma nature et Amour veulent que je me paisse."

Vos propos sont trompeurs. Si vous aviez souci
De ceux qui ont un coeur larmoyant et transi,
  Je vous ferais pitié par une sympathie;
    Mais votre oeil cauteleux, trop finement subtil,
    Pleure en chantant mes vers, comme le crocodil,
  Pour mieux me dérober par feintise la vie.

TRANSLATION

You said, my lady, as we walked alone,
    You did not care for songs of happiness;
    You loved sad songs of lovers in distress
Telling their tearful tale in tragic tone.
"Therefore," you said, "when I am on my own
    I choose your saddest sonnets, which express
    The melancholy nature I profess,
For Love himself would have me feed thereon."

Deceitful words! If you had any care
For those with hearts that weep in cold despair
    You would, indeed, have all my sympathy;
        But clever are those eyes, and full of guile!
        Yes! Sing my songs! Weep – like a crocodile
Scheming to take my life away from me!

TRANSLATIONS FROM RONSARD'S 'SONNETS POUR HÉLÈNE'

Vous me dîtes, maîtresse, étant à la fenêtre,
  Regardant vers Montmartre et les champs d'alentour:
  "La solitaire vie et le désert séjour
Valent mieux que la cour; je voudrais bien y être.
A l'heure, mon esprit de mes sens serait maître,
  En jeûne et oraison je passerais le jour,
  Je défierais les traits et les flammes d'Amour,
Ce cruel de mon sang ne pourrait se repaître."

Quand je vous répondis: "Vous trompez de penser
  Qu'un feu ne soit pas feu pour se couvrir de cendre.
Sur les cloîtres sacrés la flamme on voit passer,
  Amour dans les déserts comme aux villes s'engendre,
Contre un dieu si puissant, qui les dieux peut forcer,
  Jeunes ni oraisons ne se peuvent défendre."

TRANSLATION

Standing beside the window, dear, you said, –
  Montmartre, amidst its fields, had caught your eye –
  "For deserts and for solitude I sigh;
Not for the Court! Would I were there instead!
My thoughts would follow where my spirit led;
  In prayer and fasting should my day go by.
  The shafts and flames of Love I would defy;
His fangs should never with my blood be fed!"

I answered, "You deceive yourself, who say
  Fire is not fire when it is damped with cinder.
On holy cloisters see its flames at play!
  Deserts and towns alike can Love engender;
And to a god whom even the gods obey
  Fasting and prayers are destined to surrender."

TRANSLATIONS FROM RONSARD'S 'SONNETS POUR HÉLÈNE'

Ma fièvre croît toujours, la vôtre diminue.
  Vous le voyez, Hélène, et si ne vous en chaut.
  Vous retenez le froid et me laissez le chaud:
La vôtre est à plaisir, la mienne est continue.
Vous avez telle peste en mon coeur répandue
   Que mon sang s'est gâté, et douloir il me faut
   Que ma faible raison, dès le premier assaut,
Pour craindre trop vos yeux, ne s'est point défendue.

Je n'en blâme qu'Amour, seul auteur de mon mal,
Qui, me voyant tout nu, comme archer déloyal,
   De mainte et mainte plaie à mon âme entramée,
     Gravant à coups de flèche en moi votre portrait,
   Et à vous, qui étiez contre tous deux armée,
     N'a montré seulement la pointe de son trait.

TRANSLATION

My fever grows, but yours diminishes;
    Nor, Helen, are you touched by what you see.
    You stay so cool and leave the warmth to me.
Yours is the whim and mine the endlessness.
My heart you have afflicted with distress
    That churns my blood. My wits were doomed to be,
    At the first onset, scattered helplessly,
Terrified by your glance, so pitiless!

Love is to blame – the cause of all my woe!
Who sees me naked and with treacherous bow
    Sends shaft on shaft into my soul, laid bare,
      Till he has there engraved your image, too.
    For me, for Love himself, you nothing care –
      Yet he has scarcely aimed one dart at you!

TRANSLATIONS FROM RONSARD'S 'SONNETS POUR HÉLÈNE'

Afin qu'à tout jamais de siècle en siècle vive
    La parfaite amitié que Ronsard vous portait,
    Comme votre beauté la raison lui ôtait,
Comme vous enchaîniez sa liberté captive;
Afin que d'âge en âge à nos neveux arrive
    Que toute dans mon sang votre figure était,
    Et que rien, sinon vous, mon coeur ne souhaitait,
Je vous fait un présent de cette 'sempervive'.

Elle vit longuement en sa jeune verdeur;
    Longtemps après la mort je vous ferai revivre:
Tant peut le docte soin d'un gentil serviteur
    Qui veut, en vous servant, toutes vertus ensuivre.
Vous vivrez (croyez-moi) comme Laure en grandeur,
    Au moins tant que vivront les plumes et le livre.

TRANSLATION

So that in future ages they may sing
  Of the devotion Ronsard used to pay,
  Although your beauty drove his wits astray
And chained him as your captive, languishing;
So that our children's children, questioning,
  May learn how deep in me your image lay,
  And how you only in my heart held sway –
This little 'sempervivum' here I bring.

For, just as it will keep its early green,
  Long after death I'll make you live again –
Such skill your servant has, to intervene
  And still pay tribute to your virtues then!
As great as Laura shall you, too, be seen
  While there is life in books or in the pen.

TRANSLATIONS FROM RONSARD'S 'SONNETS POUR HÉLÈNE'

Tandis que vous dansez et ballez à votre aise,
 Et masquez votre face ainsi que votre coeur,
 Passionné d'amour, je me plains en langueur,
Ores froid comme neige, ores chaud comme braise.
Le carnival vous plaît; je n'ai rien qui me plaise,
 Sinon de soupirer contre votre rigueur,
 Vous appeler ingrate et blâmer la longueur
Du temps que je vous sers sans que mon mal s'apaise.

Maîtresse, croyez-moi, je ne fais que pleurer,
Lamenter, soupirer et me désespérer;
 Je désire la mort, et rien ne me console.
  Si mon front et mes yeux ne vous en sont témoins,
  Ma plainte vous en serve, et permettez au moins
Qu'aussi bien que le coeur je perde la parole.

TRANSLATION

Your dancing feet trip lightly to and fro;
    Your face and heart you mask with equal skill;
    But I with all the pangs of love am ill,
Now hot as embers, now as cold as snow.
You love the Carnival! I only know
    The bitter truth: that you reject me still,
    That for my years of service to your will
I have not any recompense to show.

In sighs, in lamentations and in tears
All lingering hope, my lady, disappears.
    I long for death, and nothing comforts me.
        If, seeing this, you are not moved by it,
        Grant me this last petition, and permit
    My heart and tongue to cease, and not to be!

TRANSLATIONS FROM RONSARD'S 'SONNETS POUR HÉLÈNE'

Je plante en ta faveur cet arbre de Cybèle,
   Ce pin où tes honneurs se liront tous les jours;
   J'ai gravé sur le tronc nos noms et nos amours,
Qui croîtront à l'envie de l'écorce nouvelle.
Faunes qui habitez ma terre paternelle,
   Qui menez sur le Loir vos danses et vos tours,
   Favorisez la plante et lui donnez secours,
Que l'été ne la brûle et l'hiver ne la gèle.

Pasteur qui conduiras en ce lieu ton troupeau,
   Flageolant une églogue en ton tuyau d'aveine,
Attache tous les ans à cet arbre un tableau
   Qui témoigne aux passants mon amour et ma peine.
Puis, l'arrosant de lait et du sang d'un agneau,
   Dis: "Ce pin est sacré, c'est la plante d'Hélène."

TRANSLATION

For you I plant this pine of Cybele
   That so your praises may be blazoned far.
   See, here, our names and loves engraved – the scar
Increasing with the bark in rivalry.
Fauns of these woodlands that have nurtured me,
   Who dance and hold your revels by the Loire,
   Care for this plant of ours! Let nothing mar,
No summer burn, nor winter frost this tree!

Shepherd, when hither with your flock you stray,
   Trilling on reedy pipe some eclogue fine,
Tie on the tree this message, to convey
   To all who pass this love and grief of mine;
Pour over it lamb's blood and milk, and say:
   "This tree is sacred; it is Helen's pine!"

TRANSLATIONS FROM RONSARD'S 'SONNETS POUR HÉLÈNE'

Adieu, belle Cassandre, et vous, belle Marie,
  Pour qui je fus trois ans en servage à Bourgueil;
  L'une vit, l'autre est morte, et ores de son oeil
Le ciel se réjouit, dont la terre est marrie.
Sur mon premier avril, d'une amoureuse envie
  J'adorai vos beautés, mais votre fier orgueil
  Ne s'amollit jamais pour larmes ni pour deuil,
Tant d'une gauche main la Parque ourdit ma vie!

Maintenant, en automne, encore malheureux,
Je vis comme au printemps, de nature amoureux,
  Afin que tout mon âge aille au gré de ma peine.
      Ores que je dusse être affranchi du harnois,
      Mon maître Amour m'envoie, à grands traits de carquois,
Rassiéger Ilion pour conquérir Hélène.

TRANSLATION

Lovely Cassandra and Marie, farewell!
    I served three years in Bourgueil at your side.
    (One lives; the eyes of one, since she has died,
Make heaven rejoice, but earth in sadness dwell.)
In my first April tenderness, I fell
    Before your beauties, but your haughty pride
    Neither to weeping nor to grief replied.
My life lay under Fate's malignant spell.

Now, in my autumn, hapless as of yore,
I live, as in the springtime, to adore –
    Since to my years my sorrows still are true.
        Now, when from service I have earned repose,
        My master Love drives me with labouring blows
    To compass Troy and Helen win anew.

TRANSLATIONS FROM RONSARD'S 'SONNETS POUR HÉLÈNE'

Quand je pense à ce jour où, près d'une fontaine,
   Dans le royal jardin, ravi de ta douceur,
   Amour te découvrit les secrets de mon coeur,
Et de combien de maux j'avais mon âme pleine.
Je me pâme de joie et sens de veine en veine
   Couler ce souvenir, qui me donne vigueur,
   M'aiguise le penser, me chasse la langueur,
Pour espérer un jour une fin à ma peine.

Mes sens de toutes parts se trouvèrent contents:
Mes yeux en regardant la fleur de ton printemps,
   L'oreille en t'écoutant, et, sans cette compagne
      Qui toujours nos propos tranchait par le milieu,
   D'aise au ciel je volais et me faisais un dieu;
   Mais toujours le plaisir de douleur s'accompagne.

TRANSLATION

That day beside the fountain I recall,
   In the royal garden, when thy loveliness
   Made me the secrets of my heart confess,
And all those woes which did my soul appal.
I swoon with joy, as memory through all
   My veins flows on; my strength brims to excess;
   Languor is fled, and longings stir and press –
Hopes that from me one day my cares may fall.

To every sense thou didst contentment bring:
Mine eyes beheld the blossom of thy spring;
   Mine ear could hear thee; nor, as always, fell
     Silence between us as thy friend passed by.
     I soared, a very god, into the sky –
But ever with delight comes grief as well.

TRANSLATIONS FROM RONSARD'S 'SONNETS POUR HÉLÈNE'

Quand vous serez bien vieille, au soir, à la chandelle,
  Assise auprès du feu, dévidant et filant,
  Direz, chantant mes vers, en vous émerveillant:
"Ronsard me célébrait du temps que j'étais belle."
Lors vous n'aurez servante, oyant telle nouvelle,
  Déjà sous le labeur à demi sommeillant,
  Qui au bruit de mon nom ne s'aille réveillant,
Bénissant votre nom de louange immortelle.

Je serai sous la terre et, fantôme sans os,
Par les ombres myrteux je prendrai mon repos;
  Vous serez au foyer une vieille accroupie,
    Regrettant mon amour et votre fier dédain.
    Vivez, si m'en croyez, n'attendez à demain,
  Cueillez dès aujourd'hui les roses de la vie.

TRANSLATION

When, in old age, by evening candleflame,
  You sit and spin and wind beside the fire,
  You'll sing my songs and say, as you admire,
"What charms were mine when Ronsard brought me fame!"
The lady's maid who hears you thus exclaim
  Nods, half asleep, because her duties tire.
  My whispered name shall wake her, and inspire
To pay these deathless tributes to your name!

A disembodied ghost from underground,
In myrtle shades my rest I shall have found;
  While by the hearth, when you are stooped and old,
    My love, and your proud scorn, shall be your sorrow...
Trust me and live! Delay not for tomorrow!
Gather Life's roses now, as they unfold!

TRANSLATIONS FROM RONSARD'S 'SONNETS POUR HÉLÈNE'

"Il ne faut s'ébahir," disaient ces bons vieillards
  Dessus le mur troyen, voyant passer Hélène,
  "Si pour telle beauté nous souffrons tant de peine:
Notre mal ne vaut pas un seul de ses regards.
Toutefois il faut mieux, pour n'irriter point Mars,
  La rendre à son époux, afin qu'il la remmène,
  Que voir de tant de sang notre campagne pleine,
Notre havre gagné, l'assaut à nos remparts."

Pères, il ne fallait, à qui la force tremble,
  Par un mauvais conseil les jeunes retarder;
Mais, et jeunes et vieux, vous deviez tous ensemble
  Pour elle corps et biens et ville hasarder.
Ménélas fut bien sage, et Pâris, ce me semble,
  L'un de la demander, l'autre de la garder.

TRANSLATION

"Surely," they murmured in their wise old age,
  As Helen passed them on the walls of Troy,
  "Evil must come of beauty we enjoy –
Though with one glance she can our woes assuage.
But we must stop provoking Mars to rage;
  So let her husband now take back his toy!
  No blood-soaked fields need then our peace destroy,
No captured port, no ramparts under siege."

Old men! Too feeble for such high enterprise!
  Let not your foolish words the young deter.
That, young and old, ye for her sake should rise
  With all you have and are – is worthier!
Paris and Menelaus both were wise,
  One for possessing, one for claiming her.

TRANSLATIONS FROM RONSARD'S 'SONNETS POUR HÉLÈNE'

Je chantais ces sonnets, amoureux d'une Hélène,
  En ce funeste mois que mon prince mourut;
  Son sceptre, tant fût grand, Charles ne secourut
Qu'il payât la dette à la nature humaine.
La Mort fut d'un côté, et l'Amour qui me mène
  Etait de l'autre part, dont le trait me férut,
  Et si bien la poison par mes veines courut
Que j'oubliai mon maître, atteint d'une autre peine.

Je sentis dans ma coeur deux diverses douleurs:
  La rigueur de ma dame et la tristesse enclose
Du roi, que j'adorais pour ses rares valeurs.
  La vivante et le mort tout malheur me propose:
L'une aime les regrets et l'autre aime les pleurs,
  Car l'Amour et la Mort n'est qu'une même chose.

TRANSLATION

I sang these sonnets, once for Helen made,
  Even in that sad month when my sovereign died –
  His sceptre's greatness could not set aside
The mortal debt which Charles in turn has paid.
Death waited to be mourned, but still there stayed
  Love, from whose piercing dart I could not hide.
  While through my veins flowed in that poisoned tide
All memories of my liege were overlaid.

Two separate sorrows did my heart appal:
  My lady's scorn, and – secret as a shame! –
Grief for the noble king I now recall.
  The living and the dead alike I blame.
For one I yearned, for one my tears must fall;
  For Love and Death, are they not both the same?

TRANSLATION FROM CHARLES D'ORLÉANS

(1391 – 1466)

RONDEL

Le temps a laissé son manteau
    De vent, de froidure et de pluie,
    Et s'est vêtu de broderie
De soleil luisant, clair et beau.
Il n'y à bête ni oiseau,
    Qu'en son jargon ne chante ou crie:
"Le temps a laissé son manteau
    De vent, de froidure et de pluie!

Rivière, fontaine et ruisseau
    Portent, en livrée jolie,
    Gouttes d'argent et d'orfévrerie.
Chacun s'habille de nouveau;
Le temps a laissé son manteau
    De vent, de froidure et de pluie.

TRANSLATION

A cloak is taken from the year –
   A cloak of wind and rain and cold.
   His 'broidered tunic now behold,
Of sunshine, beautiful and clear.
Nor beast nor bird but you may hear
   Chanting in accents manifold,
"A cloak is taken from the year –
   A cloak of wind and rain and cold!"

River and stream and fountain wear
   Their gayest, best apparel, bold
   With drops of silver and of gold,
And all things in new garb appear;
A cloak is taken from the year –
   A cloak of wind and rain and cold.

TWO POEMS BY GUSTAVO ADOLFO BECQUER

(Born 1836)

1

Volverán las oscuras golondrinas
En tu balcón sus nidos a colgar
Y, otra vez, con el ala a sus cristales
Jugando llamarán.

Pero aquellas que el vuelo refrenaban
Tu hermosura y mi dicha a contemplar,
Aquellas que aprendieron nuestros nombres,
Esas... ¡no volverán!

Volverán las tupidas madreselvas
De tu jardin las tapias a escalar,
Y otra vez a la tarde, aún más hermosas,
Sus flores se abrirán.

Pero aquellas, cuajadas de rocío,
Cuyas gotas mirabamos temblar
Y caer, como lágrimas del dia...
Esas... ¡no volverán!

Volverán del amor en tus oidos
Las palabras ardientes a sonar;
Tu corazón de su profundo sueño
Tal vez despertará:

Pero mudo y absorto y de rodillas,
Como se adora a Dios ante su altar,
Como yo te he querido... desengáñate,
¡Asi no te querrán!

TWO POEMS BY GUSTAVO ADOLFO BECQUER

TRANSLATION

1

To hang their nests up on your balcony
  The dusky swallows will come back again;
Their playful wing-tips once again will be
  Tapping your windowpane.

But those who faltered in their flying games
  Your beauty to observe, my joy to learn,
Those who came close enough to know our names –
  No, they will not return.

The honeysuckles, irrepressible,
  Will once again your garden walls bestride;
And once more, after noonday, lovelier still,
  Their flowers will open wide;

But those resplendent in a dewy spray
  Whose drops we gazed at – growing, quivering,
Until they fell, like tear-drops of the day –
  They never more will spring.

The ardent words of love again will sound
  And in your ears will their obeisance make.
Some day, your heart out of its sleep profound
  May haply re-awake;

But silent and absorbed, on bended knees,
  As to God's altar it is meet to go,
As I have loved you... put no trust in these;
    They will not love you so!

2

Al brillar un relámpago nacemos,
Y aún dura su fulgor, cuando morimos,
¡Tan corto es el vivir!
La gloria y el amor tras que corremos,
Sombras de un sueño son que perseguimos:
¡Despertar es morir!

2

Birth is a flash of lightning in the sky,
And even while the glow remains we die –
  Life barely makes us!
The glory and the love we hasten to
Are shadows in a dream, which we pursue;
And Death awakes us!

CANCION DEL PIRATA (THE PIRATE'S SHANTY)

JOSÉ DE ESPRONCEDA

(1808-42)

Con diez canoñes por banda,
Viento en popa a toda vela,
No corta el mar sino vuela,
Un velero bergantín:
Bajel pirata que llaman
Por su bravura *El Temido*,
En todo mar conocido
Del uno al otro confín.

La luna en el mar riela,
En la lona gime el viento,
Y alza en blando movimiento
Olas de plata y azul;
Y ve el capitán pirata,
Cantando alegre en la popa,
Asia a un lado, al otro Europa,
Y allá a su frente Stambul:

"Navega, velero mío,
Sin temor;
Que ni enemigo navío
Ni tormenta, ni bonanza
Tu rumbo a torcer alcanza,
Ni a sujetar tu valor.
Veinte presas
Hemos hecho
Del inglés,
Y han rendido
Sus pendones
Cien naciones
A mis pies.

TRANSLATION

With wind astern and all sails set
And all ten guns in line
She does not cleave the waves – she flies,
The sailing brigantine!
Well-named the *Terror*, for she yet
The farthest shores can terrorize;
A ship renowned throughout the seas
For her audacious piracies!

Moonlight over the sea,
While the wind is loud in the sail,
Silver and blue on the gentle swell
Is glimmering – beautiful.
And the pirate chief in glee
Sings out, in his poop deck stride,
(Europe and Asia on either side
And ahead of him Istambul):-

"Sail on, my ship, sail on!
No weakness show!
Fair wind nor storm, no force,
No hostile ship – not one –
Shall turn you from your course
Or bring your courage low!
Twenty prizes have we made,
Undismayed
By the English fleet.
A hundred realms
Our power o'erwhelms;
They have laid their colours
Before my feet!

"Que es mi barca mi tesoro,
Que es mi Dios la libertad,
Mi ley la fuerza y el viento,
Mi unica patria la mar.

"Allá muevan feroz guerra
Ciegos reyes
Por un palmo más de tierra:
Que yo tengo aquí por mío
Cuando abarca el mar bravío,
Al quien nadie impuso leyes.
Y no hay playa,
Sea cualquiera,
Ni bandera
De esplendor
Que no sienta
Mi derecho,
Y dé pecho
A mi valor.

"Que es mi barco... (estribillo)

"A la voz de '¡Barco viene!'
Es de ver
Cómo vira y se previene
A todo trapo a escapar;
Que yo soy el rey del mar,
Y mi furia es de temer.
En las presas
Yo divido
Lo cogido
Por igual:
Sólo quiero
Por riqueza
La belleza
Sin rival.

"My ship alone for wealth I own.
My God is – to be free!
My law's the right of wind and might,
My only home the sea!

"Kings, in their blindness, make
Ferocious war,
A handful more of land to take,
A span of earth – while I possess
All that the sea encompasses,
The sea no laws shall tame for ever more!
There are no coasts
So far away,
And no flag boasts
In such proud display,
That they dare refuse
My right to fame –
And any dues
That I may claim!

"My ship alone... (refrain)

"At the cry of 'Sail ahead!'
Instinctively,
Veering with all sails spread,
See how they turn and flee!
For I am King of the Sea,
And my fury is all their dread!
When the prize is secured
I oversee
That the booty is shared
Out equally;
And I choose from this,
As my only share,
Beauty that is
Beyond compare!

"Que es mi barco… (estribillo)

"!Sentenciado estoy a muerte!
Yo me río:
No me abandone la suerte,
Y al mismo que me condena
Colgaré de alguna entena
Quizá en su propio navío.
Y si caigo,
¿Que es la vida?
Por perdida
Ya la dí,
Cuando el yugo
Del esclavo,
Como un bravo,
Sacudí.

"Que es mi barco… (estribillo)

"Son mi música mejor
Aquilones:
El estrépito y temblor
De los cables sacudidos,
Del negro mar los bramidos
Y el rugir de mis cañones:
Y del trueno
Al son violento
Y del viento
Al rebramar
Yo me duermo
Sosegado,
Arrullado
Por el mar.

"Que es mi barco mi tesoro,
Que es mi Dios la libertad,
Mi ley la fuerza y el viento,
Mi única patria la mar."

"My ship alone… (refrain)

"So! They have sentenced me to die?
Hark to my laughter!
Good luck would never pass me by!
If I ever meet hereafter
One of those who have wished me harm
I shall string him up from his own yardarm!
And if I fall…
What should life cost?
I would reckon all
My life as lost
If what remains
Is to be a slave –
A rover brave
Who shakes his chains!

"My ship alone… (refrain)

"The North Wind is the music
Made for me –
And the shaking and the jangling
As the cables rattle free,
And the booming of my cannons
And the black and roaring sea!
When thunder breaks,
And all around
The tempest shakes
The world with sound,
The dreams of sleep
Envelop me,
Lulled by the deep
Enfolding sea.

"My ship alone for wealth I own.
My God is – to be free!
My law's the right of wind and might,
My only home the sea!"

TRANSLATION FROM CATULLUS

Vivamus, mea Lesbia, atque amemus,
Rumoresque senum severiorum
Omnes unius aestimemus assis.
Soles occidere et redire possunt:
Nobis cum semel occidit brevis lux,
Nox est perpetua una dormienda.
Da mi basia mille, deinde centum,
Dein mille altera, dein secunda centum,
Deinde usque altera mille, deinde centum.
Dein, cum milia multa fecerimus,
Conturbabimus illa, ne sciamus,
Aut ne quis malus invidere possit,
Cum tantum sciat esse basiorum.

TRANSLATION

Come, let us live, my Lesbia, and love!
Give not a groat for all the grumblings of
The sour old dodderers that disapprove!

Even though setting suns can re-arise,
When once for us the light – so fleeting – dies
One never-ending night must close our eyes;

So give me a thousand kisses, a hundred more,
A thousand again, and a hundred as before,
A thousand all in a run – and then five score!

How many thousand kisses? As they grow
We'll scatter them! And then we'll never know –
Nor any churl who may his envy show –
The tally of all the kisses shared between us two!